The 4 SPIRITUAL SECRETS

by Dick Woodward

WITH ELLEN VAUGHN

1st Edition
October 2010

The 4 Spiritual Secrets
is a special publication by
International Cooperating Ministries
606 Aberdeen Road
Hampton, Virginia 23661

*i*cm

icm

The 4 Spiritual Secrets

Copyright © 2010 by International Cooperating Ministries

Requests for information should be addressed to:

International Cooperating Ministries
606 Aberdeen Road
Hampton, Virginia 23661

ISBN 978-0-9794047-2-6
Religion - Christian Ministry

Printed in the United States of America

DEAR READER,

I pray that as you read this little book,
you will experience a revelation of God and His ways
through the kind, gentle, persistent prompting of the Holy Spirit.
May His truth, contained in the Spiritual Secrets,
brighten your way, shed light on every problem,
and chase away the shadows cast by the evil one.
I pray, in the glorious and victorious name of Jesus Christ,
that the power of God will triumph
and that in every area of your life,
God will demonstrate His faithfulness
by showing you how you can be in Him,
and He can be in you . . .
and that He will make His powerful secrets a joyous reality
in your life and ministry.
Amen.

In the love of Christ,

Dick Woodward

Follow the 4 Spiritual Secrets Blog.
Go to www.4spiritualsecrets.com

TABLE OF CONTENTS

Preface

THE FIRST SPIRITUAL SECRET: I'M NOT, BUT HE IS

THE SECOND SPIRITUAL SECRET: I CAN'T, BUT HE CAN

THE THIRD SPIRITUAL SECRET: I DON'T WANT TO, BUT HE WANTS TO

THE FOURTH SPIRITUAL SECRET: I DIDN'T, BUT HE DID

THE KEY TO THE SECRETS: I'M IN HIM, AND HE IS IN ME

PREFACE

People love secrets.

We want to decipher hidden codes and unlock great mysteries. We want to find buried treasure and know the inside scoop. Whisper the word "secret" and people pay attention.

Maybe that's part of the reason that a book called The Secret became such a national phenomenon, remaining on the New York Times bestseller list for years and selling zillions of copies. Written from a New Age-y perspective, it explores unseen dimensions of the universe, how they connect with events in our lives, and how our attitudes can help determine outcomes.

As psychologist Dr. Henry Cloud has put it, the enormous success of The Secret is intriguing on two counts. First, it shows the deep longing of so many in the world: they yearn to understand the universe and its mysteries. Second, it reveals people's hunger for principles and practices that make life work.[1]

Like Dr. Cloud, I've followed the huge response to The Secret. I'm particularly intrigued by it because my pastoral ministry for the past 40 years has been centered on what I call the "Four Spiritual Secrets."

Oh, great, you say. Here comes an evangelical pastor puffing his own ideas, trying to catch the coattails of someone else's successful book. He's probably running around the country, preaching to happy-clappy crowds, trying to climb on the "secret" bandwagon.

Not really.

I'm not running anywhere. In fact, I've been stuck pretty much in one place for decades: I'm a quadriplegic. I can't even wipe my own nose. I can't do much of anything without help, except blink, think, talk, praise God and pray. I can't go outside and contemplate the wonders of the universe, or even tilt my head back to look at the stars. I'm stuck.

But here's the wild paradox. Even though I'm stuck, I'm free.

As I'll tell you later, my paralysis wasn't the result of a sudden accident. Over time, I gradually lost the use of my legs, my

---

[1] Dr. Henry Cloud, The Secret Things of God, Howard Books, New York, 2007, page v.

arms, my whole body. Believe me: it was weird, terrifying, and depressing. You do not want this to happen to you.

But an absolute miracle came out of this horrible situation: in direct proportion to the gradual but relentless onset of my *disability*, the *ability* of God has showed up in my experience. In my weakness, I have a richer, more dynamic, and far-reaching life than I did when I was strong.

Just what is going on here?

One thing, really—the gift of God's mind-blowing grace and His peace in spite of my circumstances.

That's why I am so motivated to write this book. (Actually, I can't "write" anything; rather, I'm talking to my computer, and when it is happy and the voice recognition software works, it takes down my thoughts. If the computer is having a bad day, then I'm stuck again.)

But in spite of my sometimes uncooperative computer, I'm overwhelmed by a passion to share the four Spiritual Secrets with you. They've given me supernatural peace, real joy, and a miraculous sense of purpose and meaning every single day, in spite of my physical helplessness. They are the keys to a fruitful, purpose-filled journey in this world.

And though they may sound mysterious before we decode them, that's how all good secrets are. Besides, a mystery is a secret that is eventually revealed. That's what I hope you'll discover in this little book.   Here they are:

- I'm not, but He is.
- I can't, but He can.
- I don't want to, but He wants to.
- I didn't, but He did.

In the pages to follow, we'll dig into the mysteries of these phrases. There's a lot more there than meets the eye.

Also, I want to take you through some spiritual principles that support the Four Secrets, so my friend Ellen Vaughn and I have divided this material into 21 short, easily digestible chapters. You can use this book on your own, perhaps journaling your responses to the questions Ellen has posed at the end of each chapter. You can use it in a small-group setting, building relationships with others as you explore what God has prompted us to share with you.

At any rate, the four Spiritual Secrets began to change my life years ago . . . and now, as I wind down to the end of my days, I'd be remiss if I didn't pass them on. For if they've so changed me—when I'm essentially an old dead body with a live head, lying on a bed—think what they can do in your life!

The First Spiritual Secret:

"I'M NOT, BUT HE IS"

†

CHAPTER 1

NEED TO KNOW

There's much about life that we don't learn until we need to know it.

For example, let's say we board a plane for a long flight to Europe. Many of us might well tune out the flight attendant's obligatory speech about safety measures. Sure, we've got our seat belts fastened and our tray tables in the upright and locked position . . . but we don't tend to pay a lot of attention to instructions about how to self-inflate our emergency life vest.

But what if, halfway through the flight, the pilot comes on the intercom and announces an emergency? "Folks, this is your captain speaking, and I regret to inform you that we are going to have to ditch this aircraft in the sea in approximately seven minutes. Our flight attendant has some instructions for you."

At this point you can bet you'd listen to every single word of the safety information, sitting up straight on the edge of your flotation device.

What turned you into an A student? *Your need to know.*

Every human being needs to know the four Spiritual Secrets. They are absolutely essential if you want to survive and even thrive in life's choppy seas. But most of us don't tend to realize our need until God gets our attention when bad things happen.

That's how it was for me.

Had it not been for my illness, I don't know that I would have felt such a need to really know God and His deep secrets.

But when I was downgraded from a productive, reasonably healthy achiever who ran a few miles every day to a person who was literally unable to lift a finger or anything else, that negative transformation got my attention.

If not for the worst thing that ever happened to me physically, I doubt I would have ever learned and received the mysteries of living life fully, with joy and peace, every single day. That would have been a far, far greater loss to me than the loss of my physical strength.

If you really want to be the person you were designed to be, using your gifts, making a difference, comfortable in your own skin, doing the things you are called to do, but you just can't make that happen, then it's no accident you're reading this book. It's for you.

Ellen talked recently with a hospice chaplain. Over the course of his career, he had spent many hours with hundreds of terminally ill people, comforting and encouraging them in their last days. He said that the refrain he heard most often was this: as patients reflected on their lives, they said they wished they'd used their time differently. They wished they had perceived and acted on what was really important in this life, before it was too late. They wished they'd spent more time pursuing their relationship with God, and their relationships with the people they loved.

You don't have to be on your deathbed or paralyzed like

8

me to hear God's wake-up call to focus on your relationship with Him. Please, take advantage of my pain for your gain. Take it from one who's crashed in the ocean of loss, so to speak . . . and survived with buoyancy I never could have dreamed possible. Believe me: you need to know the Spiritual Secrets!

WHAT CAN IT MEAN IN YOUR LIFE?
QUESTIONS FOR REFLECTION AND DISCUSSION

1. What occupies most of your attention each day?

2. If you had to give a title to a book about your life over the past few months, what would the title be? Why?

3. When they get to the end of life, why do so many people seem to have regrets about how they used their time?

4. Have you had a "wake-up call" or negative experience that God used to get your attention? Describe it. What did you learn?

Chapter 2

Social Zero

I was born at the beginning of the Great Depression. It was depressing.

I was the seventh child in a family of six girls and five boys. My mother wanted to become a missionary, but when that didn't work out she was determined to recruit, train and then send out 11 missionaries into the world as her replacements!

My parents didn't own a car, and they couldn't afford to put all 11 of us on one of the buses or trolleys that passed our home outside of Pittsburgh every ten minutes. So we trudged the two miles to our church, carrying our Bibles, twice on Sunday and whenever there were special meetings during the week.

When I was 11, my mother got cancer. She was 45 years old, and after four years of awful suffering, she died in 1946. My father worked as a mail carrier by day and drove a taxicab at night to make enough money to hold the family together. Since he was working all the time, he couldn't enforce discipline in the home. During the formative years of my adolescence, I was pretty much on my own.

My mother's spiritual training hadn't taken hold of my soul, so I worshiped on the football field. In my part of Pennsylvania, football was like a religion. It had actually originated near Pittsburgh, where English coal miners like my grandfather played a form of rugby that modified into American football. At my school of more than 2000 students, football was taken so seriously that if a guy made the varsity squad, teachers wouldn't flunk him.

I wasn't big, but I liked the idea of not studying.

I made the team, my competitive edge sharpened by the violent rage that simmered in me all the time. I recently saw an old photograph that was taken of me on the football field, and my face was so harsh and angry that it shocked me. I loved to take people down. I loved to put a hurt on people. I was miserable inside and didn't really care about much of anything except football (where I was rewarded for hurting people), and the few friends who could put up with my attitude.

I wrapped up high school with straight Ds. I was convinced that I had no options, no future, no hope, and I had a lot of nothing in my brain and anger in my heart. I was a zero with the circle rubbed out.

One of my oldest sisters, Lolly, had married a pastor named John Dunlap. He called me when he heard that I was depressed because I wasn't qualified to go to college. He said he knew of a Christian university that would accept me. When I told him that my grades wouldn't get me into a good reform school, he replied that this university was willing to forget the past if a person had a spiritual perspective. I asked him, "How do you get that spiritual whatever?" He told me that if I'd hitchhike to Norfolk, Virginia he would drive me to the university, a state away.

During our long car ride, John talked with me about the Gospel. My mom had told me about Jesus for years, but since her death I hadn't thought about Him much. But now, I saw myself as such a failure that my need to know God was intense.

I knew my plane was going to crash in the ocean soon.

To my brother-in-law's absolute shock, I prayed to ask Christ to take control of my life.

I'd heard my mother say countless times, "If Jesus Christ is anything to you then Christ is everything to you, because, until Jesus Christ is everything to you Dick, He isn't really anything to you!"

She had planted this idea so deeply in my mind that when I finally came to real faith, I knew I was to go all-out, into some kind of ministry. With help from my pastor brother-in-law, I was accepted, on serious probation, by that Christian university.

That's when I started to pay big time for my academic sloth in high school. I was so overwhelmed in my classes that some of my professors told me I had an inferiority complex. I knew better. There wasn't really anything complex about me. I was just plain inferior!

Many decades later I finally realized that I had what we now call a "learning disability." Since I could not perform in some areas when I was in high school, I decided that a rebel has more status among his peers than a failure. So I opted for the rebel lifestyle.

Now with a new lifestyle, I made it through college. Like many people with learning disabilities, I had to work much harder than other students in order to excel. I was in the library when it opened in the mornings and the staff had to kick me out when it was time to close at night. I also compensated for the things I couldn't do, like math and science, by accelerating my efforts in the areas where I could perform, like Bible, English, psychology, history, and speech.

I graduated in 1953 and did youth work in California for a year, spent another year in seminary in Texas, and then traveled to Norfolk, Virginia in the spring of 1955 to visit my sister Lolly and her pastor husband John Dunlap.

When I arrived in Norfolk I drove straight to their church. Lolly was just concluding a choir rehearsal. I saw a beautiful redhead in the choir loft . . . and strangely enough, I sensed a voice inside me say, "You're going to be married before you leave this town!"

When the rehearsal ended, I asked my sister to introduce me to the girl. Her name was Ginny Johnson. I learned that behind Ginny's radiant and beautiful face there was a devout and genuine faith. I asked her out, and patiently waited until our second date to propose. (I didn't want her to think I was too forward.) We married in 1956 and settled in the Norfolk area.

Getting married did not end my inferiority issues; I remained painfully shy with most people and was uncomfortable in social situations. I was truly converted to Christ, of course, but some things were missing from my spiritual and social tool kit.

Since I was in debt, needed a job, and had double majored in Bible and Psychology in college, I took a position as a social worker. In that field I knew I could love needy people—and in a sense shepherd them like a pastor—without having to face the social challenges of leading a local church.

But the situations I faced as a social worker with child

protective services were sometimes heartbreaking and absolutely horrifying . . . as I experienced one cold and bloody winter night many decades ago.

WHAT CAN IT MEAN IN YOUR LIFE?
QUESTIONS FOR REFLECTION AND DISCUSSION

1. What were you like in high school?

2. Who has played a key role in your journey of faith?

3. Can you relate to Dick's feelings of inadequacy? Why or why not?

4. What are some of the messages we get from the world around us about self-esteem, self-worth, and success? How are those messages similar or dissimilar to the Gospel?

CHAPTER 3

PAIN AND THE LOVE OF GOD

I had volunteered to be on night call, every night, for a year. I wanted to help people in need, and I figured this was a way to do it. One night I got an alert about an emergency situation in a blue-collar residential area of Norfolk. All I knew was there had been gunshots reported, and three small children, who were in the apartment at the time of the shooting, needed to be picked up by social services. I was to make sure I received the appropriate documents when the homicide detectives turned the children over to me.

I jumped into my city car and sped to the address I was given. It was a wide, trash-strewn boulevard with a donut shop on the corner, and a one-room apartment above it. I turned up my collar against the sleet as I got out of the car.

I could not believe the scene as I pushed open the apartment's narrow door. Policemen filled the room. Empty whiskey bottles littered the floor. Police officers were conferring in one corner, and in the other there was a flimsy low bed with soiled sheets. But all I could see, everywhere, was the blood. The woman's body was in the closet, her brains splattered on the shoes. The man's body was on the bed, his blood and brain matter all over the wall.

The wife had told the husband—as he lay in bed, drunk, his .357 Magnum by his side, under the sheet—that she was leaving him, and taking the children with her. She had turned her back and leaned down to slip on her shoes. He had pulled out the revolver, aimed unsteadily, and shot off the top of her head. Then he'd put the gun in his mouth and pulled the trigger again.

One police officer had taken the couple's three small children to the only spot not blotched by gore, out on the fire escape. They were huddled in the sleet, crying. I went out to them, gathered them to me, and signed the release form the officer held toward me. His hand was shaking so badly he could barely hold the paper.

The kids crawled into my car. *Oh, God*, I prayed silently. I could not comprehend the raw horror of what they'd seen. *Please, somehow, pour Your love into the awful wound of their pain!*

All these years later, I can still see that spattered apartment. I can still feel the kids piled in the car with me like cold, frightened puppies. I knew I couldn't begin to meet their need . . . but I was taking them to someone who could.

No, I couldn't drive them over to see Jesus that night. But I took them to one of His people.

There was a woman named Mabel, a big, comfy, matronly-looking lady whose house smelled like hot biscuits and fresh laundry. Mabel was a believer, and she was one of our foster parents on call. I rang her doorbell, stomping the sleet from my boots onto her welcome mat. I ushered those stiff little kids into Mabel's warm, bright home.

There weren't any obvious miracles. But Mabel just flung her big arms wide, and those cold little children ran right to her, burying their heads in the folds of her clean apron, weeping and hugging her for all they were worth . . . and I knew I was seeing something supernatural. I was seeing how the love of Christ really does fill up ordinary human beings—the Mabels of this world—and can actually comfort those who have endured unspeakable hurt.

Much, much later, as I drove slowly home, it was almost sunrise. As the dark sky began to glow with light, I felt something I'd never felt before. It was like an electric current. It was like power from somewhere else coursing right through my body. It made my heart race. It was like liquid love.

It was wild. I knew I was no great saint or mystic. But I had experienced a profound taste of the nature of God . . . and it was clear to me that faith wasn't just some intellectual belief or nice rules for clean living. It was a *relationship* with an actual person, a Person who came to the places of greatest need and hurt. He wasn't an idea in my head . . . He was way outside of myself, way beyond what I could comprehend or imagine. But He wasn't remote. He drew near to me, and then, through Mabel and me, drew near to those kids.

The Apostle John wrote that God is love, and if we will dwell in His love, we will dwell in God and God will dwell in us (1 John 4:16). As a social worker, for the first time in my life, I experienced in a *tangible* way this God Who is love.

That night in Norfolk I discovered where God is . . . and I discovered where I wanted to be for the rest of my life, connecting the love of God to the pain of hurting people. I desperately wanted to be a conduit of His love.

As I moved toward that great calling, I still had a lot to learn.

For one thing, God would show me how to overcome my shyness and interact with people in some pretty basic social situations, like having dinner with a lovely and gracious couple . . . without throwing up!

1. What did those orphaned children probably feel on that awful night? How was God's love made real to them in such a horrible situation?

2. Have you ever been the recipient of God's love, expressed through other people, in a time of great sadness or need? How did you feel?

3. Have you ever experienced being a conduit of the love of God? Describe what happened, and how you felt.

4. Are there hurting people in your life right now? Are you willing to ask God to make you an instrument of His love for them? How will doing that inconvenience you? How might it change your life?

Chapter 4
BROKEN WINGS

In time the church of which my brother-in-law was the pastor asked me to interview for an associate pastor position. I was teaching a large adult Sunday school class of three or four hundred people. I was so shy that after class I'd hurry to an office in the educational wing of the church, where I could hide. But my teaching itself was very well received, and I was hired as an associate pastor.

Soon after, Ginny and I were asked to visit a young couple. The wife had trusted Christ but her husband, a naval officer, had not. The church leaders wanted us to have dinner with them so I could, as they put it, lead the husband to the Lord.

We picked a date, and after Ginny and I arrived at the couple's home, the wives went to the kitchen, chatting easily. Sweating bullets, I sat down in the living room with the naval officer, who was a buff, confident graduate of a prestigious university. His name was Mickey, and he was a really nice guy. But I was so intimidated by him that I felt dwarfed and inferior.

We went back and forth with strained small talk. Hatching a migraine headache, I was sweating, chalk-white, and nauseated. Mickey saw I was in a bad way.

"Do you feel all right?" he asked.

"I think I'm about to have a cerebral hemorrhage!" I stammered. My younger brother had recently had a cerebral hemorrhage, and as far as I was concerned I was about to suffer the same fate.

The officer laid me down on the couch, loosened my polyester tie, and brought a cold, monogrammed washcloth for my fevered brow. My head pounded even worse as I realized that here I was, commissioned to lead this guy to Christ and here he was, turning into my nurse.

In the end, Ginny and I had to leave the little dinner party before dinner was even served. We barely made it out of the neighborhood before I pulled over, jumped out of the car, and lost my cookies at the curb.

This little episode did not bode well for my future as an evangelist.

But as it turned out, the next day Mickey went to a meeting of the Officers' Christian Fellowship. He was friends with some of the attendees, a group of naval officers who met weekly for a Bible study at lunchtime. During the meal Mickey said, "Some guy came to my house last night to tell me something, but he was so nervous I thought he was having a stroke! Do you have any idea what he wanted to tell me?"

Mickey's fellow officers told him about the Gospel and the love of Christ, and he opened his heart to faith right there, at lunch. So this brother was indeed "led to the Lord," as the church leaders had hoped . . . but not by me!

As you can tell, I spent a good part of my early faith journey as a reluctant, confused, and even rebellious disciple.

I have learned, though, how God responds in amazing ways when we humble ourselves and determine to live life as He designed it. Christ wants every one of His followers to live lives that reveal His breathtaking ability. But we have to really want and need God enough to activate that power.

Many believers cannot take flight spiritually because they have a broken wing or two. Long before I lost my physical strength, I, too, had broken wings. I needed to know and really learn the Spiritual Secrets so I could heal and function as a human being, a believer, and a pastor.

Before I learned and experienced the Spiritual Secrets, I was a self-conscious inmate in a prison of shyness. But I was about to get sprung from behind bars, in a big way, a way that would set me free forever.

What Can It Mean in Your Life?
Questions for Reflection and Discussion

1. Did God use Dick in Mickey's life? How does this little story show that serving Christ is a team sport?

2. Dick's lack of confidence made him do some crazy things, and it's pretty ironic that he went from being an "inmate in the prison of shyness" to being a mega pastor and local celebrity, as you'll see as you read on. Are you an introvert or an extrovert . . . i.e., do you get your energy from being alone, or from being with other people? How does God use both types of people for His purposes?

3. Can you think of any areas of your life in which you are not free? What's holding you back?

CHAPTER 5

SEARCHING, SEEKING

O nce upon a time a wealthy young man decided to spend a winter in Bermuda. He had his Mercedes convertible shipped there in advance of his visit. But when he arrived on the island, he discovered, to his dismay, that the speed limit in Bermuda was 20 miles an hour.

For several weeks he cruised at that speed all over Bermuda in his powerful sports car. One morning, while driving behind an old man on a moped, he just lost it, hit the passing gear and at a speed of 45 miles per hour passed the old man. To his surprise the old man shot by him on his moped. Instinctively, he hit the passing gear and went up to a speed of 55 miles per hour. Again the old man shot by him. He accelerated and at an enormously reckless speed for Bermuda passed the moped. The old man shot right by him on his moped for a third time.

When the young man realized what he was doing, he took his foot off the accelerator and coasted to a stop on the shoulder of the road. The old man pulled in behind him and just sat on the moped, twitching a little.

The Mercedes driver approached the moped man. He was amazed at the speed the old guy had had. "Hey," he said, "what kind of power plant have you got in that bike?"

The old man couldn't speak for a few minutes. When he could finally get a word out, he said, "It's not the power plant in this moped, son. My suspenders were caught on your bumper!"

A lot of people today don't seem to have their own spiritual power plant. So they attach themselves to the bumper of those who do. They then experience spasmodic bursts of spiritual acceleration as they try to ride the energy of those they admire, without ever having found a spiritual power source of their own.

Well, here's how I got off the moped and into the Mercedes, so to speak. Here's how I got the power.

During my early years of pastoral ministry, when I wasn't busy throwing up and battling inferiority, I was struggling with deep questions about the actual reliability of the Bible. When I was in college I'd been influenced by a liberal theologian who discounted the authority of the Scriptures. He didn't see it as absolute truth, but as a fallible document whose relevance changed with changing times.

I wrestled endlessly with my doubts: *If I could not trust the Scripture, how would I know where I could find truth?* I earnestly wanted to fully trust God's Word, but at that point in my God journey I just couldn't. I was stuck. Here I was, a pastor on the staff of an evangelical church, and down deep I had doubts about the actual inspiration and authority of the Bible.

That church decided to plant a satellite church in nearby Virginia Beach, and I was asked to be the founding pastor. I was still shy, especially in large groups of people who were having spiritual cocktail parties. I functioned much better with a small group of people I knew well. There were only 20 adults who wanted to start that church, so John Dunlap thought I would work better and be more comfortable in that setting.

After moving to Virginia Beach, I met a man who owned an

oceanfront hotel that closed at the end of the summer tourist season. He gave me a key to a room, and for weeks during that fall and winter, I went to that empty hotel. I was alone in the quiet except for the sound of the surf pounding the beach outside, and I read the Bible from Genesis to Revelation, trying to decide if the Bible was truly the Word of God.

I found some verses in the Gospel of John that were the lenses through which I read. Jesus prayed, "Sanctify them by Your truth. *Your word is truth*" (John 17:17, emphasis added). I was also arrested by a verse where Jesus said of His own teaching, "If a man chooses to do God's will, he will know whether my teaching comes from God or whether I speak on my own" (John 7:17).

I had heard the liberal intellectual I admired saying, "When I *know*, then I will *do*." But in these profound verses, I heard Jesus saying, "When you *do*, then you will *know*." I decided to cast my lot with Jesus and approach the entire Bible the way He told us to approach His teaching.

I discovered that there are two views of the inspiration of the Word of God. Both are correct, but one is more mature than the other. The first view is: "The Bible is true because the Bible is inspired." The second view is: "The Bible is inspired because the Bible is true."

To show the difference between these two views, consider one more teaching of Jesus. He said that it is more blessed to give than to receive. Since the word "blessed" can be paraphrased as "happy," Jesus is saying that there's more happiness in giving than there is in receiving.

I discovered in my own marriage that if I was married to Ginny for what I could *receive* from her, rather than what I could *give* to her, our relationship became sterile and empty. But if I was in that relationship for what I could give to her, it transformed my experience as well as hers.

Since I was counseling married couples in my pastorate, I'd give them an assignment. I'd tell them that for one week they were to be in their relationship, not for what they were going to get, but for what they were going to give. I explained that if they were in the marriage for what they could get out of it, neither one would receive anything since neither one was giving anything.

When they would come back a week later, couples would often tell me ecstatically that this one idea had revolutionized their relationship. I told them there were 500 teachings of Jesus in the Bible. Since that one had shown itself to be so true, I had 499 more I would be happy to share with them!

You see, if a person holds that first view of the Bible's inspiration, you might ask them, "Do you believe 'It is more blessed to give than to receive?'" They would answer, "Is that in the Bible?" If you answered in the affirmative and showed them where that verse is found in the Bible, they would tell you they believe it.

But if they held the second view of inspiration and you asked them the same question, they would respond, "Oh, yes, I believe that because it transformed my marriage and in fact all my relationships!"

Those verses from John have remained my key to the Bible: the Bible is truth, and we should read the Bible looking for truth, with the commitment that when we find truth in the Bible we will apply it to our lives.

During that time in the ocean hotel, I read the whole Bible as thoroughly as I possibly could, looking for truth in every line, rereading passages over and over like a dry and famished person feasting on fresh, ripe fruit. I found truth after truth after truth. I'd been exposed to philosophers and great thinkers . . . but I finally became absolutely convinced that the greatest truths of time and eternity were right there in the Bible, and I wanted to share those truths with everyone I knew, for the rest of my life.

Then, one Friday morning, I found myself rereading the book of Genesis. It was so familiar . . . and yet I saw it with new eyes. I heard in a new way the questions God was asking Adam and Eve: *Where are you? Who told you? What have you done?*

I realized that some of the greatest examples of the love of God in the Bible are when we see God pursuing human beings, flushing them out of their hiding places with these questions. All the religions of the world can be summed up as man's seeking after God. But here the Bible presents a loving God Who is seeking after man.

The purpose of this story in the third chapter of the book of Genesis is not primarily to tell us what happened in the beginning, as if God owed us an explanation. It's to show us what is happening to us right now, all day long, every day. Like everything else in the book of Genesis, it's not to tell it like it was, but like it is.

So in that hotel room, I read Genesis with fresh eyes. I thought of God so tenderly seeking His people who have rejected His good order of things. I thought of His voice calling down through the centuries, looking for those who have lost their way. I knew He was calling to me, and I wept. I was so overcome with awe, wonder, and joy that I fell to my knees on the floor. And then I had an encounter with the *God who is*.

What Can It Mean in Your Life?
Questions for Reflection and Discussion

1. Where are you? Is God calling out to you?

2. What if you went to a hotel room and did nothing but read the Bible? Does that idea appeal to you . . . or does it sound dull? (We're not suggesting that you run out and rent a room, Bible in hand. The important thing in Dick's story is not the details of his particular experience, but the *results* of his experience.)

3. Where is Bible reading on your priority list? How much time do you really spend reading the Bible each day? Is there a disconnect between your answers to these two questions, i.e., the Scriptures are important to you but you spend little time actually reading them?

4. Jesus talked about people asking, seeking, and knocking . . . is your relationship with God and the Bible a passionate pursuit or a dry duty?

5. Do you have your spiritual suspenders stuck to someone else's bumper?

6. Dick doesn't apologize for having doubts about the Bible. He wrestled with his uncertainties about Scripture. Do you have doubts about God and the Scriptures? What do you do with your doubts and questions?

CHAPTER 6

BURNING BUSH AND HOLY MOSES

Normally I didn't pray out loud or kneel when I prayed in private. But I found myself kneeling and praying out loud, the hotel room filling and spilling with my joyful thanksgiving and praise. I knew the voice I was hearing was mine, but I had no idea where the words were coming from. I prayed on and on, effortlessly; I don't know for how long.

God's presence overwhelmed me with exhilaration. My insights on issues and the boldness of my requests surprised me. I heard myself praying that I might be able to teach people in all nations and languages the truths I was discovering in the Word of God. I had no idea how He would answer that prayer, but I wasn't concerned about it because I was abandoned to Him.

I felt as if God's love was surging through me like an electric current. I had already experienced the love of God passing through me on a few occasions, as when I saw Jesus' love expressed through Mabel and me for those hurting children.

But this was new. The Holy Spirit controlled me, took me beyond the sacred page, and introduced me to the living Word. It was a meeting with God, one on One, and in that meeting I was at the point where I was ready to learn the first spiritual secret that God had for me.

Nothing caught on fire in that hotel room, but it was a burning bush experience. I was on holy ground. Like Moses in his Old Testament encounter with God, I realized the absolute difference between me and the God who calls Himself "I AM."

Moses had been raised in Pharaoh's palace. He was a Hebrew, but in his life of privilege as an adopted member of the royal family, he hadn't experienced the sufferings of his people. But then one day he aligned himself with the enslaved, down-trodden Hebrews and killed an abusive Egyptian taskmaster.

He was exiled to the desert, a fugitive. For 40 years he herded sheep and had plenty of time to think. It was a far cry from life in Pharaoh's pagan palace, where he had but to utter a word and his desires were carried out. Now Moses was a nobody, spending his days prodding a bunch of mentally-challenged sheep.

We can't imagine what happened when Moses saw God in the bush that burned with holy fire but was not consumed. All we know is Moses got the point that real power doesn't come from your palace or position. Moses learned what God likes to do with somebody who has learned that he is nobody. He essentially said to Moses: "Delivering those people is not a matter of who you are, but of Who I am. You are not their deliverer. I am their Deliverer. You can't deliver them, but I can. You won't deliver them, but I will. And I'll deliver them through you! So, go deliver them, Moses!"

By application, that's what can happen when the living God shows up in our lives. What God calls us to be and do for Him is not a matter of how spiffy or talented we are. It actually has nothing to do with us, but everything to do with God and Who He is.

Moses was not the Jews' deliverer. God was. We are not

whatever we need to be to do what God wants us to do. He is. The only way we'll ever do what He wants us to do is if we are a conduit of Who and what He really is.

This is simple, so simple we can miss it all our lives. It's not about us and our identity, our self-esteem, our successes or worthiness or feelings of adequacy, inadequacy, or anything in between. It's about God, and *His* identity.

When the presence of God fell upon me in that Virginia Beach hotel room, He filled me with joy and wonder. I was overwhelmed by the love of God. Like Moses, I got hold of the first Spiritual Secret: *I'm not, but He is.*

1. How was Dick's experience of knowing he was nothing different from his earlier struggles with inferiority?

2. Have you ever had an experience of the presence of God?

3. So often we think of God living in time, just as we do. What does the name "I AM" (as opposed to "I was" or "I will be") show us about the nature of God and the fact that He dwells in eternity?

4. Do you feel like God can't or won't use you until you have your act together? If so, what does that kind of thinking show you about how you view God?

5. Have you come to the place where you are ready to learn the first Spiritual Secret?

6. What obstacles block you from experiencing the reality of the first Spiritual Secret?

CHAPTER 7

GALLOPING FREE

The first spiritual secret is so basic that it makes some people mad. "Okay," a guy once said to me. "I get it. I'm not God! It's not exactly rocket science!"

Of course it's not. We all *know* we're not God. But it's surprising how many of us spin our wheels for years, acting like every single outcome in our lives is up to us, feeling like everyone is looking to us or at us. Even though we know better, many of us feel, most of the time, like it's all about us. Egomaniacs and people with low self-esteem both do this, just in different ways.

When I finally got the point that my life as a follower of Jesus wasn't about <u>me</u>, it was absolutely liberating. Even though I had known better, for years I'd acted like being Christ's disciple depended on me being a good disciple. I'd felt like accomplishing anything for the Kingdom was dependent on me being strong and disciplined. As a pastor, I'd known that it was Jesus who saved people's souls, but I felt like it was up to *me* to be a good shepherd for my flock, or they'd all fall right off the straight and narrow path.

For example, one Saturday night I completely lost it with one of our children. I was a sweet little brown-eyed pastor, but that night I used words that hadn't come out of my mouth since I was a pagan teenager.

The next morning at church, while the choir was singing, I told the Lord in so many words, "I'm sorry, but You're out of business this morning because I had a bad night last night."

The music ended, and I stood to read the scripture I was going to preach about. The passage concerned two men who went into the Temple to pray; it's recorded in Luke 18. One is a pompous religious guy, and the other is a penitent sinner. I had never noticed before that Jesus taught this parable to those who trusted in themselves that they were righteous.

When I finished my sermon on that story, I gave an invitation, and to my surprise there were about 15 responses. I told the people I didn't think they understood what I was asking them to do. So I repeated the invitation, asking for a deeper commitment. I couldn't believe it when about 30 hands went up in response to my second invitation. I realized that God Almighty wasn't out of business just because Dick Woodward had lost his temper the night before. I realized that I was acting like God's ability to save people depended on whether I had a good night or a bad night. In other words, I was trusting in myself that I was righteous, so that the Lord could save people.

Even though I believed a theology of grace, I was living a theology of works. If I was good, worthy, productive, efficient, organized, disciplined, then I'd have a fruitful ministry. It was exhausting, intimidating, and frustrating.

But when I had my Moses epiphany, realizing that I was truly nothing, and that the Great I Am is everything, my life began to change.

First, I experienced a new humility.

Arrogant people with too much self-esteem come across as

filled with pride. It's obvious to most people around them that they need humbling. But people like I was, people who struggle with low self-esteem, are plagued by the same problem. We might seem like we're modest and self-effacing . . . "Oh, don't mind me; I'm just a dysfunctional worm!" But if you had been around me long enough, you would have realized that I wasn't really humble, because my preoccupation and focus were not truly on God (or anyone else), but on a pretty unholy trinity: me, me, and me. I may not have had high self-esteem, but I was focused on myself, nonetheless.

But when I really got the point of understanding that God had chosen me and made His presence known to me based on absolutely nothing about me, but solely on His decision to do so—and that I was really nothing and He was everything—it took my focus off me.

What a relief!

I fixed my eyes on God. I could not turn away. He is magnificent. He is love. He is awesome beyond anything I could ever imagine. Seeing even a glimpse of His glory made me see myself in proper perspective. And rather than feeling guilty or inadequate or self-focused, all I wanted to do was gaze more on Him. I truly <u>felt</u> the words of the old hymn:

Give me Jesus, give me Jesus.
You can have all this world,
But give me Jesus!

I hope this doesn't sound like I'm proud of how humble I became!

Rather, it was a distinct new <u>meekness</u> in my life. Remember when Jesus said, "Blessed are the meek" in His Sermon on the Mount? He wasn't saying that mousy, mealy-mouthed pushovers were His kind of people.

No, Christ's picture of meekness is more like a magnificent wild stallion who has been tamed. He's gifted by God with speed and strength, but he's been broken. He submits to the Master. Instead of using his energy to kick, bite, buck and rampage on his own way, he comes meekly to the Master, takes the Master's bit in his mouth, and then gallops with joy under the Master's direction.

That's the kind of humility I began to learn. I was Jesus' horse, so to speak, and I wanted to run wherever He led me.

The next gift I received from the first Spiritual Secret was a miracle: my terrible shyness left me.

Before long a spirit of boldness—not inferiority—defined me. I wasn't afraid of people anymore. It was weird and wonderful: knowing that I wasn't anything, but that God was everything, freed me from my life-long preoccupation with myself and my inadequacies.

I focused on other people instead of myself. I found out that I really loved other people, especially people who weren't in my church. I loved foul-mouthed people who wouldn't be caught dead in a Bible study. I loved alcoholics who cussed, and super achievers with Ivy League vocabularies. I was so filled up with the love of Jesus that I wanted to hang out with both down-and-outers and up-and-outers, and pass it on.

Here's an example. I had said in a sermon that believers not only could but should attend cocktail parties and then be a witness there. A friend was president of the innkeepers' association in town. He invited me to attend one of their meetings, and to be sure to come early for cocktails, so I could see what it was like to apply my sermon.

I gave the invocation for the meeting, so everybody there knew I was a pastor. As the evening progressed, the emcee and many of the people on the program got more and more risqué. Every time a dirty joke was told, everyone looked at me to see my reaction.

I was about 25 years old, younger than most of the people there, and I sat there thinking, "How did Jesus handle this sort of thing? He ate and drank with the profane people of His day, and He wasn't a wet blanket. People like that loved having Him with them."

Then I realized that *He loved the people* . . . and *they knew that He loved them.*

The mayor was sitting next to me. He'd had about 87 drinks. I thought, "Does he know that I love him?" I prayed that God would give me an opportunity to show that mayor that I loved him with Jesus' love.

Just then, out of the blue, the mayor said to me, "Padre, when I went into politics a wise old advisor told me, 'Frank, don't call 'em as you see 'em, but call 'em as they are.'

"You're obviously just beginning in the ministry, so I want to give you that same advice. Don't call 'em as you see 'em.

45

Call 'em as they are!"

I thanked him profusely and told him he had solved a theological problem for me.

"How's that?" he asked.

"Well, when I was in seminary studying the Old Testament," I responded, "it was hard for me to understand and believe the story about God using the prophet Balaam's donkey to speak for Him. It was hard for me to believe that God could speak through a jackass. But I'm absolutely convinced that God has just spoken to me through you. So now I believe that God can speak through a jackass!"

I wouldn't recommend this technique for most people, but he loved it. He threw back his head and laughed so hard I thought he was going to have a stroke.

"In fact," I continued, "You have inspired me, and I'm going to preach a sermon at our church about this."

"Okay, Padre," he said. "You let me know when you're going to preach that jackass sermon, and I will come!"

And he did. He sat in the rear corner of our little chapel—as far from the pulpit as possible--with his head down for most of the service.

I wish I could tell you that he came to faith and became an international evangelist. But I can say that this man knew without a doubt that I loved him. He became a friend. God answered the prayer that I prayed during the innkeepers' banquet.

The real impact of that innkeeper's banquet and my extraordinary conversation with the mayor was my personal realization that if God could speak through a jackass like the Old Testament donkey, and the mayor, He could speak through someone like me. And He emancipated me from my preoccupation with shyness and self. I was free to connect with people I formerly would have been intimidated by, and free to love them, really love them, with a sense of fun.

Looking back at that season in our lives, I can see so clearly that it was a rich time of miracles at home, at church, and in the community around us. I loved my life. I couldn't know then that I was about to lose a significant part of it.

Third, as you can tell from my social emancipation, I had a new sense of freedom. It was so fun to be able to wake up every day and not feel chained by inadequacy, guilt, or fear. I was at liberty to jump into my day and go wherever God led me. I was free in Him.

Fourth, I had a new, intuitive understanding of the Scriptures. This was strange and mysterious: all I can say about it was that as I read the Bible, it was clearer to me. I wasn't dependent on commentaries or scholarly analysis. (Later I returned to biblical commentaries; my library is full of them.) Remember in the Old Testament when various prophets would start their accounts with "The Word of the Lord came to" Isaiah or Jeremiah or whoever it was? I felt, in my own small way, like the Word of the Lord had come to Dick. God had changed me, and I was able to fully embrace my pastoral call to teach and preach His Word.

As you can tell, these supernatural consequences of my

encounter with God in that Virginia Beach hotel room were wonderfully life-changing.

But I am sorry to report to you that I had not achieved total sanctification. As my family would be quick to tell you, I was still a fallen human being. There was no happily-ever-after ending after the first Spiritual Secret had its way with me, otherwise this little book would be done, and you could move on to something else.

No, there were plenty more challenges to come. After the first Secret, my life would take on highs I never could have dreamed . . . and then I was struck down to a low that I'd never imagined, even in my worst nightmare.

WHAT CAN IT MEAN IN YOUR LIFE?
QUESTIONS FOR REFLECTION AND DISCUSSION

1. Do you struggle with pride, inferiority, or both?

2. Why was Dick's discovery that God could use him, even
   when he messed up, so liberating? Did it mean that Dick
   could just do whatever he wanted, and God would use him
   anyway? What could a similar discovery (or re-discovery) in
   your own life look like?

3. Has the virtue of "meekness" appealed to you in the past, or
   were you like the rest of us and thought it was kind of wimpy?
   How does Dick's description of the stallion alter your under
   standing of Jesus' view of meekness?

4. In terms of advertising, movies, music, media, and books, how does the culture around us reinforce our natural tendency to keep our eyes on ourselves? What practical steps can we take to keep ourselves from conforming to the world in this way?

5. What is your sphere of influence right now, i.e., who are the people whose lives you touch? Do they know that you love them with the love of Christ? Are there people who intimidate you, or people you don't know how to connect with? Why? How might Jesus interact with them?

The Second Spiritual Secret:

"I Can't, But He Can"

✝

CHAPTER 8

CHANGES, NO CHANGES, AND TOO MANY CHANGES

For six years, attendance at our little church increased modestly, but then growth stopped. Thereafter, year after year, we had about three hundred each Sunday. As a pastor I tried everything I could think of to stimulate the church's expansion, but nothing worked. There we all were, the same holy huddle, week after week, same old faces, same old me. It was so discouraging. I wasn't expecting to have a mega church and catapult to national fame, but I really did want our church to grow. It just wasn't happening.

The pastor who had planted the church had started a tradition of using the New Year's Eve three-hour service to give a report of all the miracles that had happened in the church during the old year, and to get the people excited about all the wonderful miracles that would occur in the New Year to come. I had gamely carried on that tradition, but I dreaded it each year.

So during this particular December, as I thought about New Year's, my problem was obvious. Nothing much had happened, really, in the old year. Everybody seemed to know that nothing supernatural was going to happen in the New Year either. In fact, come to think of it, during all my years as pastor of that church, nothing truly miraculous had ever happened, unless you count someone like me showing up to preach every Sunday.

"Why?" I moaned to God. "What am I doing wrong? What am I not doing right?"

He didn't answer, or if He did, I couldn't hear what He said.

I knew that pastors are supposed to be full of faith and have a cheerful attitude, but I couldn't stand the thought of standing up and spinning another New Year's Eve miracle report to encourage the troops.

Then, on December 31 of that year, something unusual finally happened. On the afternoon of my thirteenth New Year's Eve at the church, I was driving and heard a radio news commentator speculate about the coming year: "It's going to be the year of more of the same all over the world—more wars and more troubles, everywhere!"

I almost crashed the car. "No!" I cried to God. "Not another year like last year!"

Since my experience with God in that beachfront hotel, He and I had built a very open and honest relationship. So I continued, "If You give me another year like last year, You can take this church and stuff it. I'll quit!"

As far as I could tell, God did not have an immediate response to my threat. He was probably off consulting with pastors whose churches had had miraculously fruitful ministries that year.

Later that day, as I finished preparing my annual "miracle message," a verse from Jeremiah gave me a shred of encouragement and hope:

"Ask me, and I will tell you some *remarkable secrets* about what is going to happen here." (Jeremiah 33:3, *The Living Bible*

Paraphrase, emphasis added).

Bring those secrets on! I thought. I desperately wanted something extraordinary to happen in my church. I couldn't stand another year of more of the same. Maybe the Lord was about to answer my prayers! Perhaps, since my church seemed to be stuck in a Dick Woodward-sized rut, I'd get a call to become the pastor of a really big congregation, or maybe there would be some exciting speaking opportunities.

Well, I was about to experience something new, all right, but not quite what I'd imagined.

Early in the New Year, Ginny developed troubling physical symptoms. We started seeing doctors, and by the time that year ended, she had been in the hospital for four separate two-week stays. The doctors were stumped. First they thought she had rheumatic fever and treated her accordingly, but her symptoms persisted. Next they believed it must be rheumatoid arthritis. Wrong again. Dermatomyositis, a hard-to-spell disease that inflames and weakens the muscles, was the next incorrect conclusion.

It didn't matter what the physicians tried. Ginny became more crippled. My incredible, energetic wife, who could beat me at tennis, looked like a ninety-year-old arthritic. The last thing the doctors came up with was the possibility of a severe allergic reaction to sulfa drugs she had taken. They were scrambling. One conclusion all of them did agree on, however, was that Ginny's crippled condition was irreversible.

The months rolled on. Ginny had always taken care of our

family's domestic duties. It wasn't that I didn't want to help, but I was busy being the pastor of our church, searching diligently for miracles to report to the congregation. I was all thumbs when it came to being Mr. Mom.

The daily chaos at home was alarming. By now we had five young children, three toddlers and two still in diapers. I wished growth in our church could match the growth in our family! Ginny's crippling pain was so debilitating that she couldn't even change a diaper or give a bath.

I was clueless. The diapers were the worst. Pampers and other disposables didn't exist yet, so the dripping, soiled diapers had to be rinsed, washed, dried, and folded. Those rubber pants you put over the diaper? I kept losing them! The whole scene *stunk.*

Women in the church brought us dinner every night for nine months, even on weekends, and every morning at 9 a.m., someone showed up to baby-sit so I could go to work. You'd think this kindness would have made me grateful, but it only frustrated me more. I was supposed to be ministering to my people, not having them take care of my family and me! I didn't know how to be on the receiving end of things.

One unforgettable Saturday night, I was in the nursery, in the midst of a terrifying double diaper change when the phone rang. It was a person who was either deaf or absolutely insensitive to the fact that the kids were screaming. I wasn't prepared for the next morning's sermon, and this person—despite the howls in the background—wanted to talk all night.

As I hung up the phone all the stress and anger of being Mr. Mom along with my failure as a pastor boiled over and I just lost it. Thankfully, I got the babies into their cribs . . . then I crashed on the nursery floor and wept uncontrollably. Through my tears I gave God an earful: "What happened to that wonderful year I was supposed to be having? This isn't what I had in mind! God, I've given it my best shot for 13 years, but *I just can't do this!*"

That was the first time I'd ever said "*I can't*" to God—about anything!

WHAT CAN IT MEAN IN YOUR LIFE?
QUESTIONS FOR REFLECTION AND DISCUSSION

1. Have you ever come to the end of your rope, like Dick, realizing that you are just plain unable to do what you're supposed to be doing? Describe the scene. If you haven't experienced that, does the idea of saying "I can't" seem weak to you? Why or why not?

2. Do you ever feel like other people seem to have it all together? Do they?

3. Have you experienced any miracles lately?

4. Why is it hard for some people to accept help?

5. We live in a high-achieving, can-do culture. What happens to people who say, "I can't"?

6. What do you think Dick meant when he said, "I can't"? After all, he survived the double diaper change; we presume he got up from the floor and went on to preach his sermon the next day. What was his experience on the nursery floor about, really?

59

CHAPTER 9

How Desperate are you?

So there I was, crumpled on the nursery floor, sobbing like a baby. In my desperation I finally heard the voice of God. I sensed Him saying to me, "I've been waiting 13 years to hear you say 'I can't.' Now, let Me show you something: *I can*. I am God. I can do remarkable things, and I can do them through you!"

There it was—a gift. The second Spiritual Secret: *I can't, but He can*.

I'd been tired and frustrated before. I'd known that I was flawed and weak. But I don't think I had ever truly come to the end of myself, to the point where I actually cried out, "Oh, God, I *can't*!"

I think I'd bought into the idea that I was supposed to be able to do good things. I carried around a lot of "I shoulds" in my head. "I should be a good dad. I should be a good husband. A good pastor. A good Christian." Whatever that was.

Now, my study of the Scriptures told me that apart from Christ, I could do nothing. But I was still thinking and acting as if living as a committed disciple of Jesus Christ was dependent on <u>my</u> ability, and if I was just motivated, organized, and efficient enough, I could do it.

But that night on the nursery floor, I finally, truly realized that living as a follower of Jesus isn't just difficult. It's impossible. I could not do it on my own.

Earlier, in the breakthrough of the first Spiritual Secret,

61

I had known and experienced the fact that I *was* nothing. My identity was solely in Christ. Now I was breaking through to the fact that I could *do* nothing on my own. My actions were solely dependent on Christ.

Through my tears on the bedroom floor that night, I was saying to God, "I'm not the kind of person who can build a church!" "In fact, I *can't* build a church!" And God was saying to me, in a holy way, of course: "Relax. Jesus Christ is the One Who is building His church. Believe Me; He knows you can't build His church. But He can build His church and He can do that through you!"

WHAT CAN IT MEAN IN YOUR LIFE?
QUESTIONS FOR REFLECTION AND DISCUSSION

1. What kind of "I shoulds" do you carry around in your head? How do they make you feel?

2. Through the first Secret, Dick realized he *was* nothing. With the second Secret, he realized he could do nothing. Why the distinction? What's the difference between being and doing?

3. Marathoners will tell you that they run with patience, and that their muscles are relaxed as they run. How do we really "relax" in our run with Jesus? How does He really work through us so it's not us doing stuff, but Him doing it through us?

CHAPTER 10

PETER ROCKS

I'm so glad that Jesus chose Peter to be one of His apostles. Not only does Peter give a lot of comic relief to the New Testament, he also gives hope to people like me. When I finally came to the end of my rope and admitted that I just couldn't do what God was calling me to do, I began to see that this second Spiritual Secret is gloriously apparent in the crazy life of the Apostle Peter.

Jesus was out walking next to the Sea of Galilee one day. The breeze caught His robe; He shielded His eyes from the sun as He saw two brothers casting their net into the water. They were Peter and Andrew, weathered fishermen who, with their partners, James and John, the sons of Zebedee, were about to embark on the greatest adventure imaginable. But they didn't know it yet. (See Matthew 4:18-20.)

"Come," called Jesus, "follow Me, and I will make you fishers of men."

We don't know their entire conversation. Given his personality, Peter was probably annoyed at having his fishing interrupted by some landlubbing rabbi.

But Jesus' words had power. Next thing we know, Peter and his partners in the Zebedee Seafood Corporation were closing down business. "At once," the Bible says, "they left their nets and followed Him."

Jesus was inviting these guys to enter into a relationship with Him. He had just started His public ministry, preaching

65

repentance from sin and the coming of the Kingdom of God. He was telling these two sets of brothers that if they would follow Him, He would make them fishers of men, not just fish.

This covenant was essentially a two-part deal. First, "You follow Me. That's your part." Then, second, "I will make you fishers of men. . . . that's My part."

In other words, "*you guys follow Me*. That's *your* business! And *I will make you what I want you to be*. That's *My* business!"

The historian Luke gives us more detail when he records his version of this event. (Luke 5:1-11.) The brothers had fished for about eight dark hours and caught nothing. At sunrise, while they were tired and frustrated, dejectedly cleaning their nets, Jesus was teaching such a large crowd of people that they backed Him up on the shore of the Sea of Galilee to where Peter was in his boat. Jesus got into the boat so He could have some elevation as He taught.

When the teaching session was over, He told the fishermen to go back out on the water. They were not excited about this idea. It was the wrong time of day to fish. But Peter was starting to figure out that Jesus was God and that he, Peter, was not.

"We've worked hard all night and haven't caught a thing," he told Jesus. (I've always imagined there must have been about a 30-second pause here when the eyes of Jesus met the eyes of Peter.)

Then Peter said, "*But because You say so*, I'll let down the nets."

When he did, fish from all over the lake must have rushed

the boat. The big nets overflowed with shining, squirming, silver fish. There were so many that the nets started to unravel from the weight, and Peter signaled his partners James and John (who were in their father Zebedee's boat) to come out for backup. Weighted by tons of fish, the two boats started to sink.

Peter fell at Jesus' knees. "Go away from me, Lord; I am but a sinful man!"

"Don't be afraid, Peter," Jesus responded. "From now on, you will *catch men*." (Those two words are my favorite version of what we call the Great Commission of Jesus Christ.)

Why did Peter want the Lord to go away from him? And why did Jesus tell Peter to not be afraid? Peter was a tough fishermen who'd weathered many a storm. What did he fear?

I think that Peter knew Jesus was recruiting him for a radically different life. Like me, he was afraid of being changed, afraid of the ministry. I'm convinced that Peter was saying to Jesus, "You don't want somebody like *me* doing that! I can't do that! I'm a sinful man! I swear sometimes! I'm a mess! Go away from me!"

Peter needed to understand that if he was going to "catch men," it wasn't really up to him. The night before, Peter couldn't even catch fish. He *certainly* could never catch men until he learned to say, "*I can't, but He can!*"

Jesus was the Fisherman, not Peter. And Jesus knew what Peter could not yet see: that in just three years, after Jesus' crucifixion, resurrection, and return to heaven, Peter would preach a sermon so full of power and truth that 3,000 Jews from all over the world would become the charter members of the New Testament Church. As Peter observed the supernatural happenings of Pentecost, in that anointed sermon he proclaimed that the risen Christ "... Having received from the Father the promise of the Holy Spirit, He poured out this which you now see and hear" (Acts 2: 33). Peter knew who the Fisherman was on the Day of Pentecost.

Throughout the explosive growth of the church, this rough and clueless fisherman would be the means by which multitudes would come to faith. He would do actual miracles. Right up to the moment of his martyrdom, Peter proclaimed that <u>Jesus</u> was the one doing the miracles and bringing the human fish into his spiritual net. He knew that he was nothing and Jesus was everything. He knew that he could <u>do</u> nothing, but that Jesus could do everything.

I'm no Peter. But when I began to see the reality of the second Spiritual Secret, my life, like Peter's, changed forever.

WHAT CAN IT MEAN IN YOUR LIFE?
QUESTIONS FOR REFLECTION AND DISCUSSION

1. Why do you think Peter and his partners followed Jesus in the first place?

2. How is catching men like catching fish?

3. After Jesus' miracle of the full nets, why did Peter respond by telling Jesus to go away, that he was a sinful man? What did that have to do with anything?

4. What was Peter afraid of?

5. Are you ever afraid of Jesus?

6. What were Peter's strengths? Weaknesses?

7. How did God's power work through Peter after Jesus' resurrection?

8. What are your strengths and weaknesses? Do you believe that God really can use you in supernatural ways, or do you assume that He only uses other people, people who have their act together?

Chapter 11

Something Started to Happen

You remember how our church had not increased in size for years?

After the double diaper spiritual epiphany that changed me, something started to happen.

I had started a weekly breakfast for business and professional men. We'd get together at 6:30 every Thursday morning at a local restaurant. We'd have manly food like bacon, eggs, potatoes, biscuits, and sausage gravy, and then I'd teach from a short section of Scripture. Like my church, the group's attendance had stayed small for years.

But then, though I wasn't doing anything different and the menu didn't change either, the group started to grow. We had to move to a bigger restaurant; eventually about 400 men were meeting with me each week to study God's Word. Local businessmen who weren't interested at all in church in particular or spiritual things in general were coming to that breakfast every week. They called it "The Thursday Morning Happening."

Then I was invited to appear on a popular television talk show for women that aired on the Norfolk CBS affiliate. The hostess was well known and loved in the community. She invited me for a one-time guest appearance to discuss spiritual matters. Evidently we had some sort of chemistry, and she invited me back. And back again . . . for ten years!

Can you believe that the same man who was so shy he became nauseated and catatonic at the thought of talking about

Christ with one man was now sharing the Gospel with hundreds of men, and tens of thousands of viewers on television, in the context of a secular talk show for women?

I can't either.

Many women who watched those telecasts heard me talk about the "Thursday Morning Happening." They told their husbands to check it out. Similarly, men at the breakfasts would tell their wives to tune in to the TV show. Each of these ministries contributed to the growth of the other.

(A few years into our television relationship, the TV hostess as well as her husband and daughter, came to faith in Christ. Their spiritual journey was an unfolding miracle, brought to our entire community courtesy of the local TV station.)

The best miracle that happened, though, was that Ginny got well! She had a severe reaction to shots that had been given her for arthritis. The injections caused a high fever for 12 days—and as best we can understand, that fever seemed to burn out the crippling effects that the doctors had said were irreversible. Over a period of several months, her symptoms disappeared. She regained her strength. And though I had improved my dubious domestic skills, I was thrilled to be able to throw myself wholeheartedly into ministry at the church.

But now I was doing so in a different way than I ever had before. I had learned that I really *couldn't* do ministry in my own strength. I was looking to God in all things, actively depending on Him, and watching Him do what I could not do on my own.

WHAT CAN IT MEAN IN YOUR LIFE?
QUESTIONS FOR REFLECTION AND DISCUSSION

1. Why does God sometimes do miracles of growth and blessing, and sometimes not? What's up with that?

2. What do we learn during bad times that we wouldn't necessarily even notice during good times?

3. What season are you in right now? Feast or famine . . . or a mixture? Based on Dick's insights, what do you think God might be teaching you?

The Third Spiritual Secret:
"I Don't Want To, But He Wants To"

✝

CHAPTER 12

INCH DEEP, MILES WIDE

Throughout the decade after I told God "I can't" and He replied, "Yes, but I can," my ministry flourished beyond what I could have imagined. By the last Sunday in that New Year that had started so dismally, our sanctuary was jammed! I had worked alone, without even a paid administrative assistant, for 13 years. Now our church had multiple services and a staff of 13. My long, lonely dry period of fruitless frustration became a distant memory.

After so many years of perceived failure, I was so excited I didn't want to miss out on a moment of what God was doing. I couldn't wait for the alarm to go off in the morning. Many times I didn't, and got up at 3:30 a.m. to start my day.

Today Ginny and I look back on this time as "the decade of miracles." I had begun it relying on God's power in a way that had transformed my ministry. Unfortunately, as the years progressed, I got caught up in the lifestyle of a mega-church pastor. I rarely took a day off. I ran from meeting to meeting, full of energy, loving the ministry God had given me, but as time went on I became about an inch deep and many miles wide.

I spent too much time giving out the Word of God, and too little time taking it in. I didn't spend time communing alone with God, meditating on His Word, and listening for His voice. That would take too long. I was studying the Scriptures, all right, but always toward the end of preparing a sermon or a talk, seldom for the sake of Jesus speaking into my life, asking me those questions from the book of Genesis that had once so riveted me.

On the surface I appeared to be the sweet, little brown-eyed pastor that people loved, full of peace and insight, gliding like a duck across a deep, serene pond. But if you could have seen me from below the surface, my little duck feet were paddling a mile a minute.

I'd not lost all the intimacy of my relationship with God. I still had enough sense to say, "I can't, but He can!"

But then I would look at my watch and think, *I'll give God five minutes, and if He doesn't, I will!*

Looking back on this outwardly productive but inwardly withering season of my life, I'm reminded of writer Dallas Willard's words, "In religious matters, nothing fails like success."

One Sunday morning Clyde Taylor, head of the National Association of Evangelicals, spoke in our church. My itinerary for the week was printed in our church bulletin, and before he left town Dr. Taylor said something like this to me: "Son, I've never seen you before, and Lord knows I'll never see you again this side of heaven, but I simply have to confront you with something. You couldn't possibly do all this speaking that's listed here in your schedule and have anything from heaven for the people to whom you speak."

Dr. Taylor let that sink in, and then he continued.

"When you read the Gospels, you find Jesus either with people ministering, or He's out on some mountain in prayer. He was not always available to everybody, and He taught His apostles to come apart to a quiet place and rest awhile."

Dr. Taylor was right. I wasn't spending time recharging my spiritual batteries through a current connection with Jesus. God was still causing me to be fruitful . . . but I wasn't wholly in Him.

But when Dr. Taylor and others like him were trying to talk to me, it was as if I was in a plastic bubble. I could see their lips moving, but I could not hear what they were saying.

God was good. Life was good. And then one summer morning about ten years after my diaper-change epiphany, life changed in a bad way.

I had become a fervent runner, which was a good metaphor for my lifestyle back then. I'd leap out of bed, jump into my running shoes and shorts, and run seven miles before breakfast. Someone gave me a warm-up suit with the words "Temple Maintenance" emblazoned on the back, and I was a familiar sight out on the trails and sidewalks of Virginia Beach.

But one day when I was out for my early morning jog, I was overcome by weakness. My legs wouldn't obey my brain's orders. I was spastic.

Within a little while, though, I was okay, so I shrugged it off.

Over the next few months, it happened again and again. One time I was trying to run, my legs jerking and trembling, not getting much of anywhere, and a stranger stopped his car and asked if he could drive me home.

I declined his kind offer, rested for a while, and my body

recovered. Each time I'd suffer one of these weird attacks, the effects would slowly go away, and life could go on as usual. So I ignored my temple's flashing warning lights, and kept my life running on fast forward.

What Can It Mean in Your Life?
Questions for Reflection and Discussion

1. A lot of pastors and other leaders can relate with Dick's ex
   perience. Sadly, statistics show that many spiritual
   leaders burn out. Why is a busy lifestyle so conducive to
   burnout? What are the antidotes to a miles-wide/inch-deep
   way of living? What might the Dutch priest Henri Nouwen
   have meant when he said that "nothing conflicts with the love
   of Christ like service to Christ?"

2. Why does success so often cause us to become spiritually
   shallow?

3. What is the definition of success in the secular world? How is it similar to or different from the Bible's perspective on suc cess? Are you defining your own success—or lack thereof—based on Scripture or on the culture around you?

4. When things are going well, do you assume God is pleased with you? When your life is a mess, do you assume God is punishing you? Where do you really get your concepts about God and His perspective from?

CHAPTER 13

WHY ME?

If you ignore the warning lights on your car dashboard long enough, your vehicle will not just continue on its merry way. You'll run out of gas, or your lack of oil will create so much friction that your engine will burn up or blow up, or your brakes will fail, or some other disaster will bring you to a halt.

That's what happened to me. I was out of gas. Spiritually, I'd been running on empty for a while, and then my physical symptoms followed suit. Like a lot of pastors who spread themselves too thin without spending intimate time with God, I burned out.

Eventually Ginny and I moved to Williamsburg, Virginia, with an invitation to get involved in a new church plant that was just getting off the ground. Since my physical challenges and limitations were obviously on the rise, and I wanted to have more time to work on a survey of the whole Bible, it seemed like a good fit.

In spite of our slower pace, my symptoms persisted. The founding elder of the church in Williamsburg encouraged me to have a checkup at the Mayo Clinic in Minnesota. After almost a month of testing I was diagnosed with multiple sclerosis. (Seventeen years later I would learn that my illness was not MS, but a degenerative disease of the spinal cord.)

The disease slowly took away my strength and mobility. Within about five years I had totally lost the use of my legs and suffered from chronic fatigue. I was in a wheelchair. A paraple-gic. I could not believe it. Clearly, my most productive years of ministry were over. My dreams seemed dead.

I was devastated. For two years I wrestled with God over all the "Why me?" questions. Like so many who encounter loss, I went through the usual stages of dealing with my situation.

First I was in denial. When I could still walk, I'd push myself and act like I was okay. I'd walk so far from my car that I couldn't walk back, and I'd end up stuck somewhere, too proud to ask for help.

One time I borrowed a friend's car that had a manual trans-mission, and I got so weak and spastic that I had to manually manipulate my left leg to work the clutch. I could barely drive. I decided that if I got the car back to my friend in one piece and if I was still alive, I'd finally admit that I had a physical problem.

Then I got angry and depressed. When I saw healthy people out jogging I would feel like sticking my fist through a wall. I desperately wanted to run, and I couldn't. I'd scream and seethe inside.

At this point Paris Reidhead, a pastor friend and mentor, visited me. He asked to see my schedule for the day. "Is this what you believe God wants you to do today?" he asked, looking over my appointments.

"Yes," I said. "That's why I wrote it all down."

Looking at my exercise plan, Paris asked, "Do you have to run seven miles to do what God wants you to do today?"

I had no answer.

"Instead of being angry about what you can't do," Paris continued, "something you in fact really don't <u>have</u> to do, why not get on your face and thank God that you can still serve the Lord by preaching and teaching His Word, earn a living and support your family?"

His wise counsel helped me for many decades as I continued to lose my faculties. When you suffer a loss, you have two choices. You can focus on what you've lost and be grieved, angry, and depressed, or you can focus on what you still have and be filled with gratitude.

After my denial, anger, and depression phases, I started bargaining with God. If You heal me, then I'll do forty-eleven things I believe you want me to do.

Well, we all know that that doesn't work.

Finally, after about two years, the Lord gave me the grace to accept my situation. It was a form of inner healing. Though I had prayed once a week with a group of pastors for my physical healing for many months, I found that my inner healing deepened to the point where I didn't even pray for my physical healing anymore. When we held healing services with an Episcopal church in Williamsburg, I'd sit in my wheelchair, laying my hands on the heads of people with illnesses, fervently praying for *their* healing . . . but I no longer prayed for healing for myself.

Somehow, my acceptance was so complete that it washed out the denial, anger, and depression I had felt before. Since the inward person is a greater value than the outward person, inner healing is a greater value than physical healing. I believe God has done a far deeper healing in my soul which few people can see; it's a greater miracle than the healing of my body would be, which everyone could see.

Please note that I'm not saying this is the case for everyone; this is just the conclusion that God led me to in my particular situation.

Meanwhile, my grandchildren were a bit confused about my disability. When two of them were about three and five, we heard the older one whisper to the younger, who was pretty precocious, "What's wrong with Granddaddy?"

"I don't know," the younger one said. "I think it's leprosy. But I don't know anything about that. I haven't had it yet."

As a young man, I had been passionate about achieving two life goals. One was to start and build a great local church. By God's power—not my own—I'd seen that happen in our church in Virginia Beach.

The second goal was my life dream. Dysfunctional and inadequate as I was, I knew God had gifted me as a teacher. I dreamed of putting together a practical, devotional study of the entire Bible. I wanted it to be so clear, simple, practical and relevant that even people who didn't know the Scriptures would be drawn to it and want to study God's Word. I wanted all types of readers to experience the life-changing truths I was discovering in the Bible. I called my survey "The Mini Bible College."

My former college Bible professor and mentor—the great scholar Dr. J. Vernon McGee—visited me several times during my Virginia Beach pastorate. I shared my Mini Bible College dream with him. After reviewing some work I'd done on the book of Philippians, but hadn't finished because I was so busy, he chided me: "Why don't you get serious about this and finish the job?"

Well, J. Vernon McGee had written incredible Bible commentaries. "Why should I do this?" I asked him. "You've already done it!"

"Yes," he said. "But I'm a theologian. You're a street talker! We need to put the hay down where the cows can get it!"

Dr. McGee was a down-to-earth scholar, and he knew that most people needed a practical, plain-spoken Bible overview. He was right. Not to offend the men attending the Thursday morning breakfasts, or the women who had watched the weekly television show, but they needed the hay of the Word, right where they could reach it! That's what Dr. McGee was so good at . . . and I strove to do it too, as his disciple.

As a busy, healthy achiever and mega-pastor, my Bible study dream had come to nearly nothing after 20 years. Even though it was a great goal and a calling on my life, as the busy pastor of a large church, I never got around to working on it in a serious and thorough way.

Why? I was undisciplined. Prior to my disability, I behaved as if I believed activity equaled productivity. I was too busy "doing stuff" to have the deeper devotional life required to write such a Bible course. I was a fruitful disciple of Jesus Christ, but I believe now that God wasn't satisfied with the quality or quantity of the fruit my life was producing. As Dr. Martyn

Lloyd-Jones said, the gifts of the Spirit make us fruitful, but they do not necessarily make us holy. That was the case in my life. I wasn't holy. I wasn't set apart, pursuing God. I was running after other things.

And so here I was, so disabled I couldn't even walk, my tail bolted to a wheelchair.

Now what?

What Can It Mean in Your Life?
Questions for Reflection and Discussion

1. Dick briefly described the stages of response to his illness: denial, anger, depression, bargaining, and acceptance. Have you experienced these in response to loss in your own life? Are you stuck in one of the stages? What would it take for you to move on? Do you want to move on?

2. What are the obstacles to the profound "inner healing" that Dick experienced? Have you experienced a similar sort of spiritual restoration after a tough challenge?

3. Is there anything that you know you are called to do that you in fact are not doing? What's stopping you?

4. What keeps you busy? Is your life bearing lasting fruit, or are you, as Dick describes, too busy "doing stuff" to even see the things that God has prepared for you to do, things whose im pact will last forever?

CHAPTER 14

THE STRANGE EXCHANGE

Okay, as I said, the real reason I hadn't put together the Mini Bible College material was my lack of self-discipline.

I just plain didn't *want* to spend the time it would take to write that comprehensive Bible overview. I wanted to run and run and run. I wanted to meet with people, speak at prayer breakfasts, appear on television, and talk to people in bars about Jesus . . . all great things, of course. But they weren't what God was specifically calling me to do, and in pursuing them instead of the Mini Bible College, I was being disobedient.

You remember the biblical story of Jonah? Like me, Jonah was obedience-challenged. God told him to go preach to Nineveh, the capital city of Assyria, the greatest enemy Israel ever had. This was like asking a Jew in the early 1940s to go to Berlin and preach against the evils of the Nazis.

So it was understandable, humanly speaking, that Jonah basically responded by saying, "I don't want to." I wouldn't have wanted to either.

Jonah seems to have forgotten just Who he was dealing with. He tried to run away from God. He got on a ship headed the opposite direction, as far from Nineveh as he could get, according to the maps of his day.

God, being God, didn't lose track of Jonah. He caused a huge storm to engulf Jonah's escape vessel. The pagan sailors were so petrified that they became believers. Jonah told them to toss him into the sea, apparently preferring to die rather than obey God.

God sent a creative rescue vehicle, a huge fish that swallowed Jonah like he was a dot of plankton. Swishing around in digestive juices for 72 hours, Jonah decided to agree with God. The great fish burped, and Jonah became sea monster vomit. That was a tough way to learn a good lesson.

As you know if you read the short book of Jonah—which is worth reading, believe me—our hero went on to obey God. He still didn't want to go to Nineveh, but he knew that God wanted him to go to Nineveh. So Jonah went.

He was probably quite a sight, bleached and smelling like God knows what from his inner tour of the big fish. I'm sure he raised a few eyebrows and offended a few noses in Nineveh. But then the cruel, skeptical, pagan people of that great city repented of their great evil and turned to God.

Incredible!

God has given us, like Jonah, the freedom of choice. In a sense, He won't make us do anything. But He will put us in the belly of a huge sea monster until our only reasonable option is to choose to obey. Our lack of desire is overcome. Like Jonah, we can learn the third Spiritual Secret: *"I don't want to, but He wants to."*

It's a strange exchange, one that gives us a life-defining sense of mission, vision, purpose, and freedom. God gives us His ability in exchange for our disability. He gives us His will when we give Him ours.

The Bible puts a huge emphasis on the alignment between our will and the will of God. Jesus' greatest prayer was, "Not My will, but Your will be done." He taught us to pray, "<u>Your</u> kingdom come. *Your* will be done in earth—or in our earthen vessels—as it is in heaven."

God will not violate our freedom of choice, but He loves us enough to lean on us like an elephant until the only reasonable choice we have is to do His will. I am of course not suggesting that any physical suffering in this life is a "punishment" from God for disobedience . . . far from it. We can't know the mysteries of why God allows illness and suffering. All I know was that in my particular case, God cut me back physically so that I might bear more spiritual fruit.

My advancing disability meant that I could no longer run and run and run. Yet God was calling me to realize my dream. I had experienced in my life that "*I'm not, but He is,*" as well as "*I can't, but He can.*" Now I was actually ready to learn how God's will—His "want to"—could turn around my "want to."

Through my severe limitations, God was making me an offer I could not refuse. He wanted to show me that it was time for me to do some things for Him the way He wanted them done. He didn't toss me into the digestive tract of a large fish, but He fastened my bottom to a wheelchair.

As a result, I had plenty of time to work on my Bible course. We had moved to Williamsburg by this time, and the church there was very gracious with my time. For the next five years, I was able to devote 40 to 60 hours a week to developing the Mini Bible College. We held services twice on Sundays, had a midweek service and I spoke at two men's Bible study breakfasts during the week, but my preaching and teaching flowed out of the intense Bible study—a complete Bible survey for lay people—that I was writing. It equipped people with powerful truths for living as followers of Jesus.

The night before His crucifixion, Jesus connected with His apostles in a way that shaped their souls forever. Talking with them in the garden, He took hold of a vine with branches that were filled with clusters of fruit. You guys are like these branches, He told the apostles. My Father, the Gardener, prunes branches so they can produce even more fruit.

Two thousand years after Jesus taught His apostles that truth, I could see its tender yet painful process in my own life. I was a branch needing a significant cutback. He pruned me, if you will, so He could work miracles in me and through me. He had plans I couldn't have dreamed of. This may sound sanctimonious, but it's true: today, I don't consider my paralysis as a setback. It's a cutback, the tough but loving action of a loving Heavenly Father, designed for my good and for the greater good of many others.

Isn't it intriguing how God works? Even when we try to run away from His will, He will find a way to motivate us to get the job done. Maybe that's true in your life. Maybe you feel like Jonah, trapped in the intestinal tract of a large sea creature. But you're not trapped. Don't think God can't get you where you need to be.

Remember: Even when you don't want to, *He wants to.*

WHAT CAN IT MEAN IN YOUR LIFE?
QUESTIONS FOR REFLECTION AND DISCUSSION

1. Jonah 2:8 says "Those who cling to worthless idols forfeit the grace that could be theirs." When you think honestly about your life, are there any "idols" you're clinging to? They're probably not graven images, but are there things that occupy and obsess you, distracting your attention from God? If so, what grace might you be forfeiting?

2 Has God gotten your attention by means of crises?

3. Can human beings change for the better when things are going well, or do we only change when forced to?

4. Why did God give us freedom of choice?

5. What don't you want to do that God is calling you to do?

The Fourth Spiritual Secret:

"I Didn't, But He Did"

✝

CHAPTER 15

TEAM DOIS

Y ou've probably heard the fictional story about Jesus
talking with angels when He arrived back in heaven
after His death and resurrection. The angels are full of wonder. Fire ripples off their massive wings as they contemplate
the mysteries of Christ's work on earth. One says to Jesus—in
angel language—"This is too wonderful! What is Your plan for
this great news to be spread all over the dark planet? How will
Your Church be built down there? How will the Good News be
passed on? How can we help?"

The angels are flabbergasted when Jesus tells them He's left
all that in the hands of His disciples, who had shown themselves
to be somewhat less than reliable.

"Well, what's your plan if they don't come through for
You?" the same angel asks.

Jesus responds, "*I have no other plan!*"

It's incredible. Jesus has left the work of building His
Church in the hands of flawed human beings like you and me . . .
through the power of the Holy Spirit.

As I've already written, until my disability made me slow
down, I accomplished little in realizing the dream that became
the Mini Bible College. But when God got my attention and I
got serious about writing it, He also brought a friend and brother
into my life named Dois Rosser. Dois would fan the flame of my
dream so it would spread to places I couldn't have imagined.

I first met Dois when I was teaching the Bible to that

Thursday morning men's group. A successful businessman who owned automobile dealerships and extensive real estate developments in Virginia, Dois was one of those mover-shaker guys who slipped in each week. He attended for some time before I even met him, and then one day Dois invited me to have lunch with him at a restaurant called Strawberry Banks.

Let me set this in context for you.

Back when I had my beachfront hotel epiphany, and I prayed without knowing where the words were coming from, I had asked God that I would be able to share the great truths I was discovering in His Word with people in other languages and cultures. Over the years, regardless of what else was going on, I believed that God would one day make that happen. When I was driving to Strawberry Banks to meet Dois for lunch that day, I somehow knew that God was setting things in motion for that prayer to be answered . . . 17 years after I'd prayed it.

Dois was a good Presbyterian who had been in church all his life. He told me that God had used my teaching style to open up the Scriptures in brand-new ways for him. He was so excited about God that his priorities were turning upside down. He had an incredible sense of urgency, wanting people around the world to hear God's Word and come to faith in Jesus.

Financially comfortable, Dois easily could have sailed and played golf every day for the rest of his life. But he wanted to invest his time, energies, and money in things that would reap dividends for eternity. He decided to take his fortune and invest it in the work of building churches, orphanages, and schools in developing nations everywhere.

As a shrewd businessman and strategic thinker, Dois could see that the key to changing volatile, needy nations wasn't through top-down policies, but through the transformation of individuals, communities, and regions through the power of God. He started a group called International Cooperating Ministries as a tool for God's work around the world.[2]

Dois and I were—and are—so very different in personality and life experience. But God knit our hearts together in a way that neither of us could have dreamed. God made us partners in the work of building up His Kingdom, and He brought a lot of other people into our partnership as well.

Serving Christ isn't a solitary thing. It's a team sport. As I came together with Dois and so many others, it reminded me of my days playing football—but, happily, without the anger and violence. Each of us had our position to play, so to speak. We were committed to following our Coach's game plan, and we knew that the two-minute warning whistle was going to blow at any moment, so we were filled with urgency.

Dois and others saw that my teaching time was running out. Before my condition made it impossible for me to speak in front of groups, they decided to record all my Mini Bible College studies. The result was a series of audio and videotapes on the entire Bible. It was to become the core resource for the distribution of the Mini Bible College through technologies that we couldn't even dream of back when those tapes were first made.

The course was initially 180 lectures and almost 2,000

[2] For a more thorough and exciting overview of ICM and its explosive growth, see the Resources section at the end of this book. You can read more of Dois and Dick's story, and the colorful work God is doing through ICM, in The God Who Hung on the Cross, available through www.icm.org

pages of notes. It had to be presented in written form so it could be translated for distribution around the world . . . and again, it's safe to say I never would have written it if I had remained healthy. As it was, by the time I completed the Mini Bible College, I had gone from being a paraplegic in a wheelchair to being a totally paralyzed quadriplegic, unable to even lift a finger to turn a page of a Bible. I lay like a sack of laundry in my hospital bed, using a computer with voice-activated software.

The Mini Bible College is now 782 radio programs or studies that are translated and broadcast in 26 languages in 60 countries all over the world, with more languages and countries being added all the time. These teaching sessions are also recorded on small, solar-powered audio digital players—I call them "God pods"—that are used in thousands of small-group studies, everywhere from remote, dusty villages to teeming mega-cities. Printed guides and 33 commentaries supplement these studies. If people have access to the Internet, they can enter our website at www.minibiblecollege.org. Since all these studies are in the public domain, they can be heard, read, and downloaded at no cost.

As I write, small groups in 14, 000 villages in India are using the God pods of the Mini Bible College in India's eleven major languages. Believers in China, Rwanda, Congo, Vietnam, Cambodia, and Iraq are hearing the Word through the Mini Bible College. People are coming to faith through it in Peru, Pakistan, Sudan, and Haiti. When I started writing this Bible study so long ago, the Soviet Union was the "evil empire," an atheistic communist bloc. Today the USSR is history, and the Mini Bible

College is being broadcast in places like Russia, Ukraine, many former Soviet bloc countries, Mongolia, and Bulgaria. I am ecstatic with joy to see how God is using it.

One of the eight Chinese pastors who translated the Mini Bible College into Mandarin thanked me one day, in tears, for making this course of study so simple. (Since I couldn't come to them, these Chinese pastors were kind enough to come to my home.) They told me that though there are of course many well educated people in China, the great majority of the 1.4 billion people there have had little formal schooling. These pastors had been praying for a Bible study written at the literacy level of a 12-year-old. I considered it a compliment when they told me the Mini Bible College was the study they had been praying for—a Bible overview that an average Chinese peasant could understand.

I think the providence of God is like a Hebrew word: you have to read it backwards. Looking back from the finish line of my life, I can see God's hand in so many events. Now I believe that even my frustrating learning challenges as a teenager were God's way of sensitizing me so I could one day shape the Mini Bible College into something simple enough for educationally disadvantaged people everywhere to understand.

In addition, I saw that God's promise to me from Jeremiah--the words I had read on that dismal New Year's Eve so many years earlier—was coming true: "Ask me, and I will tell you some remarkable secrets about what is going to happen here" (Jeremiah 33:3 LB). God had had remarkable secrets for me—

the Four Spiritual Secrets! I never could have imagined how
He would reveal them to me over time and through suffering—
nor would I have wanted to know—but now I can see how the
mighty secrets He gave me have not only transformed my life,
but to my immense shock and awe and joy, they are going forth
all over the world.

As I said, God showed me that His work is a team sport.
When He wants to do His work through us, God sends us people
who have the gifts we don't have—and vice versa. Team Dois
helped me record my course of study. Later, the multimedia out-
reach of the Mini Bible College enhanced Dois's church building
strategy to the point where his team, in partnership with believers in dozens of nations, has built more than 3,500 local church
buildings across the globe.

I've also seen how God has used the Mini Bible College
to invigorate believers and draw non-believers to faith. Years
ago a wealthy lawyer named Charles Smiley started teaching the
MBC survey to a Sunday school class in the Presbyterian Church
he attended. It took him seven years to teach through the whole
thing. He taught it again, and when it was completed seven
years later, he had figured out he didn't want to do it again in that
location, so he trained others to teach it.

Then Charles and his wife Antoinette went to Cambodia,
where they've been training local pastors in the Mini Bible College. Like Dois, this lovely, well-to-do, retired couple could be
playing golf and relaxing, slightly bored, at the country club.
Instead they've been off in the wilds of Cambodia for years,

teaching the Bible to pastors who can't get enough of it, and having the time of their lives.

Eddie and Grace Liu owned a Chinese restaurant in Williamsburg. (Eddie has a PhD and was a NASA engineer and Grace has two master's degrees. They ran the restaurant on the side.) They were not believers. When the Mini Bible College was translated into Mandarin, I casually asked Eddie and Grace if they'd look at it to make sure we were getting a good translation.

Bit by bit, the Bible got into Grace and then Eddie. They came to faith. They sold their large home and moved to a smaller place near the College of William and Mary campus, and today their passion is for Chinese students at the college. They bring them to their home for dinner every Friday, and after dinner they all study the Bible together. Because of Eddie and Grace, dozens of Chinese students have come to faith in Jesus and been publicly baptized. Eddie and Grace have also been instrumental in seeing the Mini Bible College taught throughout China.

Obviously, I couldn't begin to make the Mini Bible College bear such fruit. Nor could Dois or I have ever dreamed how God would use International Cooperating Ministries in such powerful ways.

In that is the simplicity of the fourth Spiritual Secret: *I didn't, but <u>He</u> did.*

God knew I needed to get to work a decade or more ahead of time so He could have the precise materials ready for the right countries, at the right time. I believe that's why He cut me back, planted me in a wheelchair and then a hospital bed, and gave me the passion and the discipline to complete the Mini Bible College. I thank God for driving me to fulfill my dream and my call. It's in this context that I can accept and even be joyful about my limitations. I also know Who deserves all the credit for my dreams coming true in bigger ways than I could have imagined.

What Can It Mean in Your Life?
Questions for Reflection and Discussion

1. Dick says that serving Christ is a team sport. Why? How?
   Are you connected with other believers? Who's on your team?

2. Are there people in your life who can challenge and encourage
   you in your faith journey? Are you part of a local church?
   Why or why not?

3. What do you notice about the stories about the Smileys and
   the Lius? What changed their lives? How are they bucking
   the cultural norms around them? How are they connected to
   others?

4. What are your gifts?

5. Are you using them to enrich other people's lives?   Looking
   back in time, have you seen how God has used your
   abilities—and/or your disabilities—in other peoples' lives, for
   good?

CHAPTER 16

JUST A JACKASS

One November morning when the Thursday morning men's breakfast was at its peak, an international banker stood to say a few words. "As we approach Thanksgiving this year, the thing I am most thankful for is Dick Woodward--because I have found Christ at this breakfast!"

When I came up next to teach, the whole audience of men rose and gave me a long, standing ovation. I was grateful but embarrassed, too.

As you already know, I'm hot on the jackass stories in the Bible. Remember the account of Jesus' triumphal entry into Jerusalem? Jesus was riding on the back of a donkey, and people were all around Him, spreading palm branches on the path in front of Him. They shouted, "Blessed is He who comes in the name of the Lord! Hosanna!" Providentially, that very week I had heard a world-famous Presbyterian radio pastor ask the question, "When all those people were shouting all those wonderful things about Jesus, now wouldn't it have been silly for that little old jackass to think that was all for him?"

So after all those men stood and applauded at that breakfast, I shared what I had heard on the radio, and then I said, "If the Lord has spoken to you here, or if He has ridden into your life through this breakfast, thank *Him*. Don't thank the jackass!"

Even though I knew the donkey shouldn't get the acclaim, it took many more years for me to fully grasp the truth of the fourth Spiritual Secret: *"I didn't, but He did!"*

Like all the Secrets, it's absolutely freeing. It's not about us, it's about God. When He brings fruit in our lives, or when He does miracles and great things of any kind, we can't take the credit. We didn't do it. He did. We can be free to be humble and truly God-honoring. It would be pretty ridiculous for Jesus' donkey to think people were cheering for him. The same is true for us.

The Apostle Paul was no jackass. He was probably the Bible's most credentialed achiever. He was pretty relentless about his resume. He was a triple-A personality who had faultless credentials and a track record full of good works. After he came to faith in Jesus, God utterly converted his soul but maintained Paul's personality and gifts, using them for a new purpose. Paul wrote half the New Testament and put the Church of Jesus Christ on the world map. He pressed himself to do all he could for the Kingdom of God.

It would have been easy for Paul to fall into the trap of pride. While he wasn't perfect in his post-conversion life, he knew full well the power of the fourth Spiritual Secret.

In his inspired letters he writes, continuously and emphatically, that it was not he who did these great things. He wrote to the Corinthians that when he preached the Gospel and planted the church there he did so in great weakness, in fear and much trembling. He claimed that his ministry there was a demonstration of the power of the Holy Spirit. In his writings he consistently essentially states, "*I didn't, but He did.*" He ran his race full-tilt, knowing that any fruit of his work came from the power of God, not from the power of Paul.

WHAT CAN IT MEAN IN YOUR LIFE?
QUESTIONS FOR REFLECTION AND DISCUSSION

1. Why do human beings love applause?

2. How does the world around us encourage pride and self-sufficiency?

3. What does pride do in people's personalities?

4. What is the antidote to pride?

5. Why is it liberating to give God the credit due Him?

CHAPTER 17

GETTING PEOPLE INTO THE WORD, AND THE WORD INTO PEOPLE

Many years ago, back when I was mobile and before the Mini Bible College was fully developed, God gave me a foretaste of how its Bible teaching could be used to change lives.

A couple from an affluent church where I was teaching on Monday nights asked to meet with me to discuss their college-age son. He was a brilliant student, but had had a mental breakdown. They were just about to commit him to a psychiatric hospital when he told them he had had a deep spiritual experience. Since this couple had heard my teaching in which I emphasize personal spiritual experience, they thought perhaps I could help their son. They wanted to know if I thought he really did have an experience with God, or if he was just lost and delusional.

I went straight to their home. It was late, and I came in through the kitchen door. There was the son—I'll call him Mitch—kneeling on the floor, praying loudly, his arms straight up over his head as he called out to heaven.

"Oh, God!" he cried. "Send somebody! Send somebody!"

I walked into the room, and he snapped out of his prayer.

"Who are you?" he asked suspiciously.

"You've been asking God to send somebody, haven't you?" I asked him. "Well, He sent *me*!"

After talking with Mitch that night, and meeting with him a few other times, I believed he did have an experience with God.

I also believed he had many mental health challenges, and I encouraged his parents to seek professional help for him.

The night before he was admitted to a mental hospital I had a hamburger with Mitch. He told me he had been to hospitals like this before, and he knew he would have many long hours with nothing to do. He asked me if I could give him something to continue his spiritual education while he was hospitalized.

I had just finished teaching the Mini Bible College survey course, and I had all the cassette tapes in a brown paper bag. (This was a preliminary version of the material, before I got serious and wrote the extensively researched, entire survey after the onset of my disability.) I gave Mitch the wrinkled bag of tapes and assured him of my prayers for him.

Since Mitch was a brilliant biology major, he was curious and decided to check out what this preacher had said about Genesis and the account of Creation. When he heard my approach, he became very interested in the rest of the course. He started going through the whole series.

Periodically, his parents would call me and tell me Mitch had had another spiritual experience. I told them the important thing about a spiritual experience is not the details of the experience itself, but its results. They told me that yes, they could see big positive changes in Mitch's life.

By the time he had about seven of these experiences, Mitch told his family that he wanted to come home and have me baptize him. That was arranged, and I met him for lunch. I could immediately see in his eyes the healing that was taking place inside of him.

It reminded me of a verse in Psalm 107 which says, "He sent His Word and healed them." By the time Mitch was baptized, this healing was so obvious that his parents decided that he was gaining more from the Mini Bible College than he was from the hospital. (Please note that I'm not knocking psychiatric hospitals; this was just what Mitch's family decided to do in his particular case.) They signed him out of the facility, and established him in an apartment near our church. They asked me if I'd consider him an intern and continue to mentor him in the Bible.

I agreed to do this. Mitch arrived at our home, we had dinner, and then I took him to his apartment and went to our church across the street.

As I walked into my study at the church with the lights out, I could see Mitch out on the front lawn of the apartment building, on his knees, his hands up in the air. He was singing, "I come to the garden alone, while the dew is still on the roses . . ."

It was winter, and steam was coming out of his mouth.

"And He walks with me and He talks with me," Mitch warbled on. I could see the lights coming on in various apartments as people checked out what in the world was happening and I wondered if they were getting ready to dial 911.

I stood there in my dark office, staring out the window, and realized the full weight of what I had committed to do. I really prayed through the four Spiritual Secrets that night.

The intern relationship continued for more than three years.

Mitch jogged with me in the mornings and then ate breakfast with me and my family. Our kids loved him, though they were a little confused by some of his odd habits.

Eventually, as Mitch continued to heal, I persuaded him to apply to seminary. When he had finished four years of seminary with an extraordinary record and a post seminary degree, since he had not finished college, he had to return there and live in a dormitory for a summer session to demonstrate his changed behavior. It was a tough, well-respected university with a national reputation; the assistant to the president told me that after he left that school, diploma in hand, its president turned to his assistant and said, "There *has* to be a God!"

Mitch finished seminary, married, had children, received his doctorate, and has preached the Gospel all over the world. He's seen many, many people come to faith in the Middle East, India, Africa, and on college campuses all over the U.S. He has started faith-based schools in Kenya, helping some 50,000 students grow spiritually and academically. God has used him to touch thousands of lives, and those new believers have touched others, who've touched others with the love of Christ, passing on the Good News like ripples on a pond.

Mitch's summary of the principles of the four Spiritual Secrets goes something like this: "Jesus Christ plus anything equals nothing. Jesus Christ plus nothing equals everything!" He would be the first to tell you that since he came from such pain, he knows that any ministry he has is through the power of *God* working in his life . . . that he can't do anything, but God can. He's an actual, living example of the Spiritual Secrets, and the greatest example of God's healing power at work through the Word of God that I have ever personally seen in my five decades of ministry.

WHAT CAN IT MEAN IN YOUR LIFE?
QUESTIONS FOR REFLECTION AND DISCUSSION

1. Dick doesn't give much detail about Mitch's mental health challenges, and his story is not suggesting that immersion in the Bible will always heal people's neurological conditions. What risks did Dick take in developing a relationship with Mitch? What might have happened if Dick had not done so?

2. Can you give an example of how God's Word healed a broken area in your life or in the life of a friend or family member?

3. C. S. Lewis called faith in Christ "the good infection," in that it's like a virus that infects one person, who passes it on to two more, who infect four more, who spread it to eight more, and so on. How has God's touch in your life been passed on to others and others beyond them?

CHAPTER 18

HERE I AM, SORT OF

As I complete this book, doctors tell me that I'm very near completing my time on this earth.

I am quite a sight. My body is limp, a lumpy collection of skin and bones. I can think, talk, and eat, but that's about it. I cannot move my legs, torso, or arms. I have chronic pain from the continuous dead-weight pressure on my sciatic nerves. I tell people I have TB: Tired Butt. I've actually had Botox injections in my gluteus maximus; doctors hoped they might relieve my terrible pain. Unfortunately, they didn't work, but you'll be happy to know that I have fewer wrinkles down there than I used to.

I've been housebound now for 15 years. When it became apparent that my strength was diminishing and that God was most likely not going to heal me physically, Team Dois and other friends built us a new, handicapped-friendly home. It's really a miracle that I'm still alive . . . a testimony to the incredible, nurturing attention of my wife, my care-lover, over so many years.

The only times I've left home over these years have been in an ambulance. Once recently I was vomiting black blood and my heart was just about to stop. On several occasions I've simply not woken up, causing no small stir among my loved ones when they've tried to shake and rouse me from 6 a.m. until late in the afternoon when I've finally woken up in the hospital. Our neighbors are used to the sound of sirens and the roar of emergency vehicles coming to rush me to the hospital.

Yet even though I lie here in a heap, unable to scratch my nose, let alone move my torso and legs, my mind sprints and my heart is ablaze! I cannot stop thinking of our wonderful God, and I lift up constant praise for all He has done. I'm amazed at how he has used a man with a weak and broken body like mine to influence people—not just near my home in Virginia, but all over the world.

As my life winds down, I spend my days in a hospital bed in the living room. A machine circulates air through the mattress to relieve my pressure points and prevent bed sores. It sounds like my bed is breathing. Through the windows to my sunny front yard, I can see new blossoms in the spring and swirling snow flurries in the winter. Woodpeckers, cardinals, blue jays, and squirrels visit our birdhouses and trees.

We have human visitors as well, and unlike the birds and squirrels, they get to come in the house. The William and Mary basketball team has been here twice. (This year they had a very good season, but I'm not sure we can attribute that to their visits here.) A while ago the football team visited. Every week I meet with about a dozen young men, many of them on the large staff of our church. I watch them as they stride up our front walk, full of strength and life, without discernible limits in what they can achieve. I wish they could know, really know, the four Spiritual Secrets without having to experience what I've gone through. When I think of what God had to do to get me to do the Mini Bible College, I wonder what it will take to get these young people to do what He wants them to do. And I sometimes feel like the guy who told me, back when I was in my early twenties, "I am old, I'm gloriously old, and I wouldn't be as young and ignorant as you are for anything in the world!"

At any rate, I'm so thankful for these relationships. I'm so thankful that God can still use me in my weakness to challenge those who are so full of gifts and strength. I've found that these guys can be honest with me in a way that they perhaps wouldn't if I was strong and healthy.

A long time ago, I began to learn how to ask honest questions. I used to lunch with a friend on Mondays. I'd always ask him, "How are you, Skip?"

"Great, wonderful, marvelous, tremendous!" he'd answer. Always!

On many Mondays I'd not had a good weekend, and life was not great, wonderful, marvelous, and tremendous for me. But this guy was unceasingly optimistic.

After this pattern continued for some time, one Monday I asked him, "Tell me something. If everything wasn't great, wonderful, marvelous, and tremendous with you, how would you answer my question?"

"Oh, I'd lie to you," he responded.

We both chuckled nervously.

I decided to rephrase my question. I asked, "Where are you, *really*, Skip?"

He looked at me for some seconds and then came clean. He worked with a group of people who emphasized Scripture memory and they all memorized a verse each week. "Frankly, if you really want to know," he said, "My verse for this week is, 'Hang it on your beak, freak!'"

That, I could relate to.

His candor opened the way for us to have a truly honest exchange, what I call "reality contact." Ever since that conversation, I use that rephrased question when appropriate to find out what's really going on with others.

So now I want to ask you—"Where are you, *really*?" If you walked up our front walk and in our front door right now, what would your <u>honest</u> answer be?

I've discovered that with most of us, most often, God is allowing circumstances to stretch us to the limit. Have you ever had that happen? Are you there now? Is God helping you understand the four Spiritual Secrets through overwhelming problems that are forcing you to admit you don't know what to do? Even if you did know what to do, you wouldn't have the power to do it?

Does sin have you by the tail—are you afflicted with hurts, hang-ups and habits?

Are you running from God in disobedience like Jonah did?

Perhaps you're facing evil in a person or situation and are getting pushed around?

Is your heart broken because of pain in relationships, perhaps a divorce or a rebellious or prodigal child?

Are your finances a mess?

Perhaps you have a physical disability or weakness like me? Are you feeling the despair of a "hopeless" condition?

Or, like me at one time, are you in a ministry where you've learned the impossibility of trying to produce spiritual fruit in your own strength?

Maybe God is using your current need to show you that *you're not, you can't,* and *you don't even want to,* because *He* desires to do wonderful things in and through you that can only be explained by the words *you didn't, but He did.*

The bottom line is that it really doesn't matter how you ended up where you are. God is waiting for your 911 call. Do what I did. Tell Him, "I just can't."

He has an answer for you: "*I can!*"

What Can It Mean in Your Life?
A Question for Reflection and Discussion

1. Where are you, *really*?

The Key to the Spiritual Secrets:
"I'M IN HIM, HE'S IN ME"

✝

CHAPTER 19

IGNITION

A s you know from some of the stories I've shared—and believe me, there are a lot more—I'm just a little vehicle-challenged. One time my car was in the shop, and a friend loaned me his Mercedes. I was so excited about driving this heavy, luxury car with its powerful engine; I couldn't wait to see what it could do.

But as I settled into the driver's seat and tried to get going, nothing happened. The ignition was on the steering column, and I tried to turn the key over and over and over, but it wouldn't move. My fingers got red from trying to turn the key so hard.

I called the owner, and he told me the secret of how to get the car started. I didn't know that with this particular model, you had to change the gear from park to neutral to park again. Once I knew that non-spiritual secret, the key turned and the ignition system engaged, activating the combustion of fuel in the engine. The car roared to life.

It's not a perfect metaphor, but you see my point. It doesn't take much to master the four little phrases of the Spiritual Secrets and to understand their potential force. But unless you use the key for their ignition and get them in gear, you won't get anywhere. You might know what the Secrets are, but you won't know their power in your life.

Here's the key that activates and energizes the four Spiritual Secrets. *"I'm in Him, and He's in me."*

Let me explain.

If you listen to Jesus carefully as you read the Gospel of John, especially the fourteenth through the seventeenth chapters, you will discover that He often speaks of His Father and the relationship they have. He mentions the Father 124 times in the Gospel of John and 43 times in His last retreat with His apostles just before His crucifixion. Regarding the principles of the four Spiritual Secrets, in these "Father passages," we hear Jesus essentially say:

- The important thing is not Who and what He is, but Who and what His Father is.

- What really matters is not what He can do, but what His Father can do through Him.

- Jesus didn't come to earth to do what He wanted to do. He came to do the will of His Father Who sent Him.

- Jesus said that it was the power of God that made everything He did possible. He explained His relationship with the Father by saying things like, "I and the Father are one." And "Believe Me, that I am in the Father and the Father is in Me."

Jesus told His apostles that after His death and resurrection, He would send them the Holy Spirit. He showed them how His work and His words were essentially an overflow of His relationship with His Father. Because He and the Father were one, the Word of His Father was spoken on earth and the work of His Father was done on earth—through Jesus.

Jesus challenged the apostles that if they would be at one with the Holy Spirit, modeled by the way that He was one with His Father, the words of Jesus would be spoken on earth and His work completed on earth, through *them*. He also said that His words weren't just for them, but for all those who would believe in Jesus through the apostles' message, spread through centuries and generations to come.

That would be us!

"I am the Vine, and you are the branches," Jesus said. "If you will be joined to Me through the Holy Spirit the way branches are joined to a vine, you will have the power to speak My words and do My works for Me!"

Of course, if the branches aren't "in" the Vine, they can't do anything on their own. No fruit.

This applies to you and me today. Through the miracle of Jesus' resurrection and the actual presence of the Holy Spirit in us today, we can speak Christ's words and do His works. Apart from Him we can do nothing. But when we are in Him, the way a branch is in a vine, we enjoy an organic, flowing relationship that will inevitably produce fruit. We don't have to huff and puff and try and try, determinedly working to push-push-push and make fruit. Jesus will do it through us. We can relax in Him.

It's simple, but it's absolutely mysterious, and again, it's the key to the Spiritual Secrets. *I'm in Him, and He is in me.*

Many of us frequently misplace our car keys. No matter how powerful our car may be, it's useless if we don't have the key that ignites its engine. In the same way if we do not have the key to the ignition that activates and drives these Spiritual Secrets, they will not get us anywhere.

I'm indebted to E. Stanley Jones, a missionary who served

in India for 50 years, and his superb daily devotional, In Christ, for showing me the importance of this phrase in the New Testament. He says that the Apostle Paul used this phrase nearly 100 times in his inspired letters.

According to Dr. Jones, when we think about being "in Christ," we should realize that Paul was not talking about being in religion. Few people have been more into religion than Paul was before he met Jesus. Paul was so religious that he was devoutly persecuting followers of Jesus, sure that he was pleasing God by trying to snuff out the Jesus cult.

It is possible to be in religion, but not be in Christ. It is possible to be in church, and not be in Christ. We can be in doctrine, or theology, and not be in Christ. We can be in the ministry and not be in Christ. We can be committed to Christ, and believe a lot of things about Christ, and still not be in Christ.

To be in Christ locates us in a person, right *now*. We can say, "The Lord was my Shepherd," or we can say, "The Lord is my Shepherd." In the same way, we can be in alignment with Christ today and out of alignment with Christ tomorrow.

The best biblical example of that inconsistency is, of course, our buddy the Apostle Peter. One minute he's in line with Jesus, proclaiming that Jesus is the Messiah, and Christ says to him, "Blessed are you, Simon, for this was not revealed to you by man, but by my Father in heaven!" And then the next thing we read in the account, Peter takes Jesus aside to rebuke Him, and Jesus tells him, "Get behind me, Satan! You're a stumbling block!" (See Matthew 16:13-28.)

Peter was filled with God's revelation one minute and a blockhead the next. His status depended on where his focus was, on whom he was depending. We are the same way. Our alignment with God is a matter of our attitude in the present moment. Are we saying to God, "Thy will be done," actively dependent on Him, or have we slipped out of gear and we're all about "my will be done"?

To summarize and paraphrase the way the Apostle Paul wrote about his own relationship with Jesus, it was something like this: "I'm in Christ, and Christ is in me. Everything I do, I do by Christ, in Christ, and for Christ. For me, to live is Christ. I live because Christ lives in me and I live in Christ. Everything I am and do is simply all about Christ!"

How can we gain this mysterious intimacy with Jesus in our own lives?

WHAT CAN IT MEAN IN YOUR LIFE?
QUESTIONS FOR REFLECTION AND DISCUSSION

1. What does it mean to be in religion, but not in Christ?

2. What does Dick mean when he says that we can be in alignment with Christ one day, and not in alignment with Christ the next? Can you see examples of that in your own life?

3. At this point in your life, are you current in your relationship with Christ? Or has your power cord slipped out of the socket, and when you talk about faith you're basically describing a dynamic from the past, not the present?

Chapter 20

Keep It Simple

B ack when I was fighting for my theological life, having been traumatically influenced by liberal theology while in college and seminary, God graciously provided extraordinary mentors who helped me work out what I believed. To mention a few of them, these were men like Dr. J. Vernon Mc-Gee, Dr. Ray Stedman, my pastor Dr. John Dunlap, Pastor Paris Reidhead, Dr. Henry Brandt, Dr. Roy Burkhart, and Dr. Richard Halverson. All these guys have passed on to glory; I can't wait to see them again.

The liberals doubted that Jesus even existed. During my beachfront hotel epiphany, I experienced the divine presence of God. Before that experience I was giving the critics of the Scriptures the benefit of the doubt. After that experience it was the other way around, because I had *experienced* God's existence. Knowing His reality removed the mountain of doubt from my shoulders. It was not that God answered all my questions. I just had no need to ask them anymore.

Regarding those who doubted Jesus, I'd come to the place where I could say, "I believe that He is, while they're not even sure that He was. And while they're not even sure He did, I know that He still does."

A long time ago, when I used to complain to my sister Lolly, who is with the Lord now, she would say to me, "The Lord knows." It irritated me no end. It sounded like pious God-talk.

"Okay," I said to her one day, "so the Lord knows. What's

that supposed to mean to me?"

Her response was pretty simple. "We know the Lord is good, He is love and He is all-powerful. So all we need to know is that the Lord knows about our situations. If He knows, if He is all-loving and all-powerful, He will do what we really need for Him to do."

Lolly was right. Regarding my illness, I no longer need to ask, "why me?" I honestly feel that God doesn't owe me any explanation for my severe limitations. If He healed me, that would be all right. If He doesn't heal me, that will be all right too because *He is all right!* I've experienced and know that He is good, that He is love and that He can do anything. The Lord knows my needs. I'm a knotty little branch, just resting in Him, relying on His Spirit.

I think the term "Spirit filled" is so often misused today, as if there are Spirit-filled believers and then all those other believers. There are Spirit-filled pastors and then other pastors. There are Spirit-filled churches and then all those other churches. The implication is that those who are Spirit-filled are always Spirit-filled and the others are never Spirit-filled.

Sometimes when I met people in a shopping mall they would recognize me and say, "Oh you are the television talk show pastor. Are you Spirit filled?" My standard reply was, "Not always. Are you?" The Holy Spirit is a Person. We either have that person in our life or we don't. He's not a liquid and we're not a glass. The issue is not how much of the Spirit we have, but how much of us the Spirit has. The Apostle Paul helped me understand this when he wrote that we are not to be drunk with wine, but are to be filled with the Spirit. In the original language, the command is literally "to be, being filled with the Spirit." It is an ongoing, present-tense state, a continuous filling.

As a drunk is under the influence of alcohol, we are to be under the influence, or control, of the Holy Spirit. We want to yield more control to Him, just as a person under the influence of alcohol yields more control to alcohol. When we are filled with the Spirit, we are still ourselves, just as a drunk is still himself or herself. But the Spirit is evidenced in everything we do . . . just as alcohol is evidenced in everything a drunken person does.

Some people are apprehensive about being filled with the Spirit. But to be filled with, or controlled by, the Spirit is to be like Jesus.

When Jesus sent His apostles to get the donkey He would ride into Jerusalem for His triumphal entry, He instructed them that all they had to tell the owner was that the Master needed the animal. The disciples would then discover that it was available.

God does not use super-duper people to do super things because they are super people. He delights in doing extraordinary, supernatural things through ordinary people who are available. What God is actually looking for today are little old donkeys that are available to their Master. Whether we are an illiterate fisherman like Peter, or a highly educated rabbi like Paul, *our greatest ability is our availability*.

I've lived near a major seaport for more than 50 years, and

I have known many nautical people. I've learned from them that when a large ocean vessel is ready to dock in a port, the captain doesn't sail his own ship all the way to the pier. Instead, specialists called "harbor pilots" perform this delicate task. They're experts at berthing large vessels and know everything about the harbors where they work.

There was a man who was one of the oldest and best of these pilots, but he had a peculiar habit. Every morning before leaving for work, he went to a wall safe in his family room and removed a little black box. Carefully opening the container, the old harbor pilot took out a small sheet of scrolled white paper and read it reverently. Then he returned the scroll to the box, put the box in the safe, closed the door, and spun the lock.

His wife, who had seen her husband do this every day for years before he left for work, frequently asked him, "What's written on that little scroll of paper?" The man would smile, but he never answered her question.

Years later the harbor pilot died. After his funeral his widow was quite curious about what was written on that paper in the black box, stowed in the safe. After opening the little vault and removing the black box, she carefully took out the tiny scroll. Unrolling the yellow, crumbling paper, she was astonished to find only six words:

Port is left, starboard is right.

That old man believed in sticking with the basics and holding them in perspective.

The four Spiritual Secrets are just as basic as that to me. I don't have a safe in the wall of my family room, but if I did, and I had a little black box with a scroll inside, these words would be written on my scroll:

> *I'm not, but He is, and I'm in Him and He is in me.*
>
> *I can't, but He can, and I'm in Him and He is in me.*
>
> *I don't want to, but He wants to, and I'm in Him and He is in me.*
>
> *I didn't, but He did, because I was in Him and He was in me.*

I would read those lines every morning before I faced the challenges of the day so I would be sure I was in relationship and harmony with the Lord. Until our dying days, these four Spiritual Secrets—and the key to their ignition—will be as fundamental to Ginny and me as "port is left, starboard is right" was to that old harbor pilot.

What about you? Are you willing to plug into the power of God in your life? Will you allow your circumstances to bring about an alignment between your will and the will of the risen, living Christ? If you will, you will one day look back on many miracles in your life. And you will be filled with joy, awe and wonder, affirming that: "*He is! He can! He wants to! And He did . . . because I was in Him and He was in me!*"

WHAT CAN IT MEAN IN YOUR LIFE?
QUESTIONS FOR REFLECTION AND DISCUSSION

1. To go with Dick's reference to Ephesians 5:18—"Do not get
   drunk on wine, which leads to debauchery. Instead, be filled
   with the Spirit"—how does a person get drunk, anyway?
   What parallels are there in terms of how we get "filled with
   the Spirit"?

2. Dick says that we're all control freaks, in one way or another.
   It's hard to let go of our natural desire to manage all the out
   comes we possibly can. Is there any area of your life that
   you're holding back from the Spirit's control? Are you afraid
   of what might happen if you yield your control? What is
   control, really? What keeps you from being fully available to
   God?

3. Dick says that one of his favorite quotes—which is actually a summary of his convictions formed over decades, as a result of all the good mentoring he had—is as follows: "Jesus Christ, the Christ Who still is, because He's risen, is everything He says He is. He can do everything He says He can do. You are everything Christ says you are, and you can do everything Christ says you can do, because He is, He is in you and you are in Him." That can be kind of hard to penetrate . . . but keeping Dick's understanding of God's presence and goodness in mind, what does it mean? How could these truths change your life?

4. What troubles or confuses you about the four Spiritual Secrets?

Chapter 21

The End of the Beginning

I started this book trying to convince you that you *need to know* the four Spiritual Secrets. And that's how I'm going to end it. I would be remiss if I didn't. After all, my days are drawing to a close, and as I look over God's wonderful kindness and grace over the course of my life, I'm ready to go be with Him in glory. I believe that with this little book, my work here is done.

So take it from a dying man: you need to know the four Spiritual Secrets and the key to their power!

When I was a 25-year-old pastor, I met Linwood Jones, an older pastor who greatly influenced my perspective on the ministry. His wife had died and he had suffered a nearly incapacitating heart attack. We often fished together, and had a great father/son relationship. Depressed since his wife's death and frustrated that he couldn't work in the ministry any longer, he'd often ask me why he was still alive.

I didn't know . . . but together we figured out that God must still have had work for him to do.

Then, to Linwood's delight, he was asked to be the interim preaching pastor of a nearby church. His remaining family insisted that he get my approval before he accepted their invitation. I made him promise me that he would not get involved in their business meetings, but simply preach until they found a new leader.

One Sunday morning when he was about to enter the pulpit,

he grabbed his chest and fell to the floor like a stone. It was another massive heart attack. An ambulance rushed him to a medical center 20 miles away. I drove like a maniac to that hospital. I rushed to his room and found him looking like a little boy who had just found something wonderful under the Christmas tree. He stuck his hand through a small opening in his oxygen tent to shake hands with me.

"Dick!" he said. "I'm getting ready to graduate! Will you preach my commencement sermon?" He told me he wanted me to preach on John 17:4, in which Jesus says, "Father, I have glorified You on the earth. I have finished the works You have given Me to do."

Linwood passed on a few days later. He had been the pastor of seven North Carolina churches, and it was an enormous honor for me to lead his "commencement" service for the multitude of Southern Baptists who had dearly loved their "graduated" pastor.

Musing on Linwood's commencement text affected me deeply. I'm sure he knew it would cause me, as a young person at the starting gate of ministry, to think about my own finish line. When it was time for me to "graduate" would I be able to say, like Linwood, that I had glorified God on the earth and had finished the works He had given me to do?

In 1956 the famous missionary Jim Elliot was speared to death, along with his four colleagues, by the primitive people they were trying to reach with the Gospel. Jim was a passionate follower of Jesus Christ. About four years before he died, he wrote in his journal, "When it comes time to die, make sure all you have to do is die."

Jim Elliot had no way of knowing that he would die when he was just 28 years old. To the rest of us, it seemed like he had a lifetime ahead of fruitful work for the Kingdom. In human terms his life seemed cut short, inexplicably. But in God's terms, Jim had done what he was assigned to do, and it was time for him to come Home.

We can't understand how God decides the day of our death. We don't know when our own finish line will come. But whether you're like Jim Elliot and die young, or like me and die old, we should all live in such a way that when we come to the finish line of our life there will be no unfinished business, no works our Father assigned to us that we've left undone.

Many, many years ago, I had a rather spectacular accident in my life-long adversarial relationship with vehicles. A naval serviceman from Indianapolis had left his car with me while he was at sea. It was a custom-built, classic 1955 MG convertible, but it had a supercharged Corvette engine and many special features.

The steering failed on a curve, and I crossed over several lanes of fast traffic to hit a big orange highway truck that was coming from the opposite direction. When that huge truck hit the little MG, the accelerator stuck to the floor, my right foot was caught under the brake pedal, the doors and windshield were sheared off, and I was dragged by the car with the rear wheel peeling rubber 18 inches from my head. I hit the truck again on the opposite side as it was coming to a stop in the median between two double lanes full of traffic.

It was a miracle I survived with only minor injuries. In fact, when the side of the truck came over the top of the MG, my old football training kicked in. As defensive linemen, we were drilled that when we were going to be trap blocked, we were to drop to the ground. So when I saw that truck coming in my peripheral vision, I instinctively dropped. Instantly. If I hadn't done that, I'd have been decapitated, and you would not be reading this book.

The accident was written up in local newspapers, including the words of the first witness who was an old farmer who picked up my Bible and my sermon notes and papers that had scattered all over the highway. He handed them back to me, shaking his head with amazement that I was alive, with words I'll never forget: "Mister, either you is serving the Lord or *you'd better serve the Lord!*"

People asked me what I was thinking about while I was being dragged by that car. My entire life did not pass before me, as might be expected. Rather, my honest thought was, "Oh, Lord, please! Not now! I not only haven't finished the works you have given me to do. I haven't even found those works yet!"

It was 14 years later when I actually began writing the Mini Bible College. It was almost 30 years later when the process of translating and broadcasting the Mini Bible College into other languages and cultures was started. And it was 50 years before I would dictate these words to you via my obedient computer.

Recently a young pastor from India spent a Saturday morning with me, telling me about the wild and wonderful things God was doing through the Mini Bible College in his part of India. He told me that the pastors for whom he was responsible had very little theological education, and that his denomination was requiring the study of the Mini Bible College and my commentaries to train them in the Bible. He told me that long after I had died, my life work would still be equipping and educating pastors in India.

At the end of our time together, as we prayed for each other, he began to weep. He prayed that when he came to the finish line of his life and ministry he would be able to say, as well as I could, that he had glorified God on earth by finishing the works our heavenly Father had assigned him to do.

Naturally, his prayer made me think of Pastor Linwood Jones, and the way his life and ministry had inspired me in the same way more than 50 years earlier . . . so I was absolutely filled with gratitude and worship. I thank God for permitting and directing the events of my life that have made it possible for me to find and complete at least some of the works He's given me to do, works that will bring glory to His name.

And what lies beyond the finish line?

The Bible doesn't say a whole lot about heaven. Many of us have fluffy images of the hereafter as a sort of puffy, dull place full of fat cherubs, harps and clouds. Those inane pictures have a lot more to do with greeting cards and gift-store figurines than they do with the Scriptures. The images of heaven in the book of Revelation are stunning and mysterious. Powerful. They set our hair on end. They are strange and allude to things too magnificent for us to yet comprehend, because we think in too few dimensions.

My first clues about heaven came when I was 15 years old, and I watched my mother cross the finish line at the end of her life, when she was 49.

Our 13-member family lived in an 834 square-foot home. We were like a big litter of puppies in a box. There was very little privacy and lots of noise; my mother often lamented that she never had any peace and quiet.

But as she was dying, tucked into her bed, with all of us crowded around her, she seemed to already be passing in and out of heaven. She would exclaim, "Oh, what peace! What peace! I've never known such peace!"

Several times she started to describe certain things she was experiencing, but then she would pause and say, "But I can't tell you about that."

Back when the cancer had begun to consume her body, my mother had prayed for healing. But when it became clear that God wasn't going to grant physical healing, she was at peace. She told my father that "except for leaving you with so many [loud] children, I have no regrets. And I wouldn't change places with you for anything in your world!"

So though we grieved the loss of her, at the same time we actually envied her. The overwhelming impression I received at her death bed was that heaven is a glorious, tangibly real place, unimaginable to those of us on this side of the divide.

Now, as I lie in my own death bed, I remember an experience from my days playing high school football.

My high school represented the city of Greensburg, which had a population of about 30,000 people. We were playing against a high school that represented the city of Altoona, which had a population of 90,000. We had not beaten the Altoona team in 13 years, and on this particular occasion, we were beating them.

Our coach must have been hysterical, because he put me into the game.

I assumed my defensive position right where the ball was, and I was about to go charging after the quarterback, when the referee reached over my shoulder, grabbed the ball and raised it over his head, signifying that the game was over.

He saw the crestfallen expression on my face, and yelled through the ear hole in my helmet, "I'm sorry, son. It's over. It's on the scoreboard now!"

People were going crazy in the stands. Our victory was so astonishing and wonderful that our principal actually gave us a day off from school. I was thrilled that we won, of course . . . but I was crushed personally, because I didn't get to play.

I *almost* got to compete, but I was not part of the victory.

Ever since that experience, I've resolved that I don't want to be a spectator, sitting on the sidelines while others win the victory.

The book of Revelation tells us that we're on the winning

team, and one day God is going to pick up the ball and say, "It's all over! The victory has been won!"

But an issue we will live with for all eternity will be, *"Were we part of the victory?"*

The Apostle Paul tells us that everything we do for Christ after we come to faith is like sending gold, silver and precious stones into the eternal state. Everything we do for ourselves is like sending wood, hay and stubble into the eternal state. When we appear before the judgment seat of Christ, to have our works evaluated, He will apply fire to what we have accumulated. The fire will consume the wood, hay and stubble, but it will purify the gold, silver and precious stones. (1 Corinthians 3:12-15)

When the heavenly fire purges and reveals how we spent our time on earth, what will we have left?

In that bittersweet night before Jesus was crucified, He told His apostles that they had not chosen Him. No, He had chosen them, and would strategically place them to go and bring forth fruit that remains, or lasts. He added that when they understood this, God would start answering their prayers. (John 15:16)

We didn't choose Jesus to be in alignment with what we're doing. He chooses us to come into alignment with what He is all about. In other words, we don't decide to choose Jesus and take Jesus into our plans. He chooses us and takes us into His plans. For me, I can see that God has used all the events of my life—including my limitations, both personality-wise and physical—to take me into His plans and bring out of my life the fruit that remains.

It's incredible!

I challenge you to pray to that same end. Do you understand that He has chosen you to be His partner? Can you interpret the events and happenings in your life in that context? Because He loves you, Christ wants to bring purpose and meaning into your life by guiding you to those works He foreordained that you would do for Him when He saved you. (Ephesians 2:10)

Great purpose, meaning and joy will come into your life when you decide to cooperate with Him. You'll see Him bring fruit out of your life. I pray that you will give Him that cooperation, so you'll be filled with wonder as He makes it possible for you to one day deposit gold, silver and gorgeous jewels at the judgment seat of Christ.

You don't know when you'll get to that day. Neither do I. But it's a good bet than I'm closer to the finish line than you. In fact, I'm lying right on it. So, again, take my words with the weight they deserve, as a last will and testament from a dying man!

I've never forgotten the great preacher Henry Drummond's words, from his sermon, "What is Your Life?"

"...Your life is a transitory thing. It is a thing of change. There is no endurance in it, no settling down in it, no real home to it here. Therefore God calls it a *pilgrimage* – a passing on to a something that is to be...it is true, life is a mysterious thing. We do not understand life – why it should begin, why it should end. There is some meaning in it somewhere that has baffled every search; some meaning

153

beyond, some more real state than itself. So the Bible calls it a sleep, a dream, the wind. No book but the Bible could have called our life a sleep...

"The Bible has the profounder thought. *Life is the sleep. Death is but the waking.*"

For my part, I look forward to *waking up* . . . and I will look forward to seeing you there!

1. There is a lot to chew on in this chapter. What struck you about Dick's reflections on life, work, death, and eternity?

With Gratitude

First, my heart is filled with grateful worship to God, without whom there would be no Spiritual Secrets about which to write!

I consistently use the editorial "we" since I can do nothing without the help of my precious wife Ginny. Everything I do is only possible because she is at my side 24/7. I write by talking to my computer, using speech recognition technology. Though this technology is a miracle, the system is not perfect. Countless times every day I must call for her assistance—and she is always there.

I'm grateful to a long list of godly people God placed in my life who mentored me into the discovery and application of these four spiritual absolutes. As I reflect on how God taught me these truths, I am so grateful for the spiritual communities of devout brothers and sisters who learned them with me.

I greatly appreciate the help of those who were kind enough to read this in manuscript form and offer feedback and suggestions: Janice Allen, Craig Falwell, Mike Cook, Gloria Pratt, Lee Vaughn, and Laura Warren.

I thank God for Dois Rosser, who shared my passion to teach the whole Word to the whole world and put together a team of people God used to make that dream a reality. The vision, faith and sacrifice involved in that miracle verified and confirmed the four Spiritual Secrets in my life and ministry.

I want to thank Bruce Nygren, who encouraged me to write about the Secrets. Bruce graciously worked with me on an earlier draft, and I'm grateful to my sister Helen Swiner, who, among others already mentioned, helped to review it. My gratitude knows no bounds for Mark Christensen, who challenged me to try again at a time when I had given up on this project, and also presented a draft of how this manuscript might be written. The technology I have used to write this manuscript would not be in place if it were not for the faithful mentoring of David Schweikert, who has spent 2 hours with me every Friday morning for 14 years to teach me this technology.

My heart overflows with gratitude to Ellen Vaughn, who used her great gifts as a writer to put a window into a message I have been trying to communicate in writing for more than two decades.

I express my gratitude to all who helped me focus the message of this book in this team sport spiritual secret:

I couldn't but we did—in Christ!

$\mathcal{D}$ick Woodward

In the late 1970s, when his mega-church ministry seemed at its zenith, **PASTOR DICK WOODWARD** was afflicted with a rare degenerative disease of the spinal cord that slowly and steadily left him a bedfast quadriplegic. In spite of huge obstacles and crippling limitations in his life, he became an internationally well-known, locally successful, and beloved mentor, pastor, and Bible teacher.

Dick is a husband, father of five, grandfather of five, great-grandfather of one and has been a pastor since 1956. In 1956 he founded Virginia Beach Community Chapel where he served as senior pastor for more than 20 years. In 1979 he joined the team of those who started the Williamsburg Community Chapel where he served for 15 years as a pastor and now as Pastor Emeritus. He had a popular TV program and a nationally-aired radio program for many years and he taught hundreds of men weekly for 20 years at breakfast Bible studies.

Dick received his B.A. degree from Biola University and did graduate work at San Jose State University and Dallas Theological Seminary. He is the author of many devotional and inspirational booklets and the author of a uniquely clear, devotionally practical, systematic and expository survey of the scriptures, known as the Mini Bible College (MBC), which is an integral part of International Cooperating Ministries' (ICM) strategy.

As a ministry, ICM is deeply committed to spreading the Good News of Jesus Christ throughout the world by empowering Christian leaders with MBC materials to nurture their own people. The MBC programs are now in 26 languages spoken by over 4 billion people. These languages can be downloaded or streamed worldwide via internet, in both written and audio format, and are also broadcast into many countries. More language translations are in development or being planned.

 *Ellen Vaughn*

ELLEN VAUGHN is a <u>New York Times</u> bestselling author and inspirational speaker. Her recent collaborative books include *Choosing to SEE, Shattered, Lost Boy,* and *It's All About Him.* The last debuted at #1 on the <u>New York Times</u> nonfiction list. Vaughn has also authored *Time Peace* and *Radical Gratitude.* Her award-winning novels are *The Strand* and *Gideon's Torch,* which she coauthored with Chuck Colson. She collaborated with Colson on 9 other nonfiction books.

Former vice president of executive communications for Prison Fellowship, Vaughn speaks frequently at retreats, conferences, and writers' seminars. Vaughn holds a Master of Arts from Georgetown University and a Bachelor of Arts from the University of Richmond. Vaughn and her husband Lee live in the Washington, D.C. area with their teenagers Emily, Haley, and Walker. She enjoys reading, walking, drinking coffee, and staring pensively at the ocean. *www.ellenvaughn.com*

 International Cooperating Ministries

Mission Statement:

To nurture believers and assist church growth worldwide.

How do we do it? Two ways:

 **Mini Bible College:** ICM-Partnered churches use the Mini Bible College material by Pastor Dick Woodward, in their own language for teaching and nurturing believers in their congregation and Bible study groups as an outreach ministry of the local church.

 **ICM Church Building Program:** provides a place and presence for believers in rural areas in over 50 nations around the globe.

 ICM is a non profit, trans-denominational parachurch ministry guided by our adherence to the Lausanne Covenant Statement of Faith. ICM is a ministry of the Rosser Foundation. 100% of every designated dollar goes to its purpose in the mission field.

www.icm.org

www.minibiblecollege.org

www.tolearntolive.com

161

If
The
4 SPIRITUAL SECRETS
by Dick Woodward
WITH ELLEN VAUGHN
HAS BLESSED YOU...

Please help ICM bless believers around the world with
Pastor Dick Woodward's teachings through the

Mini Bible College

A monthly gift of $50 or more will start a new Bible study group
each month

or

will make you a member of the ICM Church Building Club.

Enclosed is my first month gift of:
- ☐ $50.00/month   ☐ $100/month
- ☐ $200/month   ☐ $_____

To be used for:
- ☐ Mini Bible College   ☐ Church Building Club

Credit Card Information
Charge my card monthly for $_____.
☐ Visa   ☐ Mastercard   ☐ American Express   ☐ Discover

Credit
Card#:_____ 3 Digit Security Code:_____
Expiration Date:_____
Signature: _____

Billing Address:
Street:_____ City: _____
State:_____ ZIP:_____
Email Address:_____

Also available in audio
To order: Visit www.icm.org, mail in or call toll-free 1-877-622-7778

Mini Bible College Products

BOOKS	for a gift of...	Qty	Total
* Mini Bible College Old Testament Handbook	$10.00		
* Mini Bible College New Testament Handbook	$10.00		
The God Who Hung on the Cross	$10.00		
The 4 Spiritual Secrets	$10.00		
A Spiritual Compass: God's Eight Great Questions	$5.00		
BOOKLETS			
30 Biblical Reasons Why God's People Suffer	$5.00		
How to be an Eagle Disciple	$5.00		
In Step with Eternal Values	$5.00		
A Prescription for Guidance	$5.00		
A Prescription for Peace	$5.00		
A Prescription for Yourself	$5.00		
A Prescription for Prayer	$5.00		
Communication: A Tool that Builds Marriages	$5.00		
Psalm 23: Sheep Talk	$5.00		
A Christmas Prescription	$5.00		
The 7 Spiritual Wonders of the World	$5.00		
Jonah: True Confessions of a Prophet	$5.00		
The 4 R's of Parenting	$5.00		
Ten Fingerprints of a Healthy Church	$5.00		
A Covenant for Small Groups	$5.00		
A Prescription for Love	$5.00		
Happiness that Doesn't Make Good Sense	$5.00		
AUDIO RESOURCES			
* Old Testament Audio CDs (Complete set)	$100.00		
* New Testament Audio CDs (Complete set)	$100.00		
The 4 Spiritual Secrets (3 CD's)	$10.00		
The God Who Hung on the Cross (5CD's)	$10.00		
New/Old Testament Audio CDs (Complete sets)	$175.00		

Gift total	Shipping
$8.99 or less	$2.50
$9.00 - $25.99	$6.00
$26 - $50.99	$7.00
$51 - $100.99	$10.00
$101 - $250	$15.00
Above $250	Please call

Total for items: _____

Shipping: _____

Taxes: _____

My additional gift to MBC: _____

My order total: _____

VA resident add 5% tax on products with *

Mail to: ICM, 606 Aberdeen Road, Hampton , VA 23661